THE OFFICIAL
COOKBOOK

THE OFFICIAL COOKBOOK

JUSTIN WARNER

INSIGHT
EDITIONS

San Rafael • Los Angeles • London

Contents

Recipes marked with ▶ *are featured in an Eat the Universe episode on Marvel.com.*

MEASUREMENT CONVERSION CHARTS

ABOUT THE AUTHOR

ACKNOWLEDGEMENTS

INTRODUCTION

Justin Warner here, and today, we're gonna *Eat the Universe*. If you aren't familiar with the Marvel Digital Series this cookbook is based on, well, start bingeing! On the series, I get the opportunity to cook foods inspired by the characters, creatures, costumes, and customs of the Marvel Universe. I am pumped to be writing this book as a companion piece to the show because now I get to be even more of a culinary ambassador to all things Marvel.

Even if you aren't an omega-level cook, there are still plenty of recipes here you can finesse with ease to match your skill level and celebrate your favorite characters. Also, unlike many cookbooks, in this one you'll have the videos available at your fingertips to help you out along the way. Just head over to marvel.com and—with the exception of a few recipes that are exclusive to this book—you can search for almost any recipe you're looking for. This cookbook is also arranged by protein type, so you can first decide what you'd like to eat, and then see what recipe piques your interest in that section.

This whole thing got started shortly after I won Season 8 of *Food Network Star*. I was introduced to Agent M (Ryan Penagos, vice president and creative executive, Marvel New Media) and invited onto his podcast to discuss food and all things Marvel. After the podcast, I mentioned that if he ever wanted to chow down on some Marvel-inspired dishes, he should hit me up. Sure enough, he did. We did a little segment about the Monsters Unleashed series in the 2010s, and I must have impressed, because after a few more test runs, Marvel invited me to be their Chef of Heroes and

Hero of Chefs (okay, I gave myself that title) and become the host of *Eat the Universe*.

I can truly say that this is the greatest job on Earth-616, and I think my enthusiasm shows. Almost every guest asks how I got the gig, to which I reply, "I am a fan." 'Nuff said, right?

Indeed, my parents encouraged me—an only child—to read at any opportunity, and Marvel comics would transport me to worlds far beyond my living room floor. If you really want to know how far back Marvel and I go, my first comic book purchase was at a drugstore that still served grilled cheese. Yes, back then drugstores had little counters where you could read your comic book and have a snack before going about the rest of your day. Perhaps this is my origin story?

Anyway, I've always been a fan of Marvel, and I even once wrote the company a letter asking them to make commercially available web-shooters. I'll also never forget my librarian's expression when I checked out books on arachnids and nuclear physics when I was about eight years old. That's how profound Marvel's effect was on me. It made me believe that if anyone was going to become something great, it could even be me. That attitude carries through in the food I make on *Eat the Universe*. Now I'm passing that Phoenix Force of can-do attitude on to you.

Hit me up on my personal Twitter or Instagram accounts for any of your culinary quandaries along the way. I'll absolutely do my best to answer. I'd love to see your edible interpretations of your Marvel favorites!

CHICKEN

Phoenix's Hot Chicken and Egg Oyakodon

**YIELD:
2**

This was the very first recipe to be released as an official *Eat the Universe* video! This awesome dish was inspired by the concept of family: Jean Grey, her Phoenix persona, and her stepson from the future, Cable. *Oyakodon* translates as "parent and child bowl," so I think it's fitting for this Marvel family. You don't have to have a techno-organic virus to make this dish, but it does help to have the right gear. Make sure you have the right vessel for frying—either a Dutch oven or an electric fryer, and always use a thermometer, lest you burn like the Phoenix Force. Oblate discs, optional in this recipe, are clear, filmy, edible sheets made from potato starch that you can purchase online.

FRIED CHICKEN:
3 cups buttermilk, divided
2 tablespoons vinegar-based hot sauce
1 tablespoon kosher salt, plus more for seasoning
4 boneless, skinless chicken thighs
Vegetable oil for deep-frying
4 cups all-purpose flour
Black pepper
6 tablespoons cayenne pepper, or to taste
4 tablespoons paprika, or to taste

SAUCE:
2 tablespoons paprika
2 tablespoons cayenne pepper
¼ cup brown sugar
2 tablespoons soy sauce
1 tablespoon mirin
½ white onion, sliced
1 cup water
1 small packet (8 to 9 grams) dashi seasoning
2 tablespoons vinegar-based hot sauce

BOWL:
2 eggs
3 cups cooked rice, warm
1 food coloring marker (optional)
4 oblate discs (optional)
Sour dill pickles for garnishing

TO MAKE THE FRIED CHICKEN:

1. Combine 1½ cups of the buttermilk with the hot sauce and the 1 tablespoon kosher salt in a nonreactive bowl or zip-top bag. Place the chicken in the bowl or bag with the marinade. Toss the chicken to coat, and refrigerate, covered, for at least 4 hours or up to 24 hours.

2. Fill a Dutch oven halfway with the vegetable oil, or fill a deep fryer according to the manufacturer's instructions. If using a Dutch oven, heat the oil to 375°F over medium heat. If using a deep fryer, set the thermostat to 375°F.

3. Divide the flour evenly between two shallow dishes or trays. In a third shallow dish or tray, add the remaining 1½ cups buttermilk. Arrange the trays of flour on either side of the buttermilk. Season the first tray of flour with plenty of kosher salt and black pepper. It's hard to overdo the salt and pepper, but if you need a measurement, let's just say 1 tablespoon kosher salt and 2 teaspoons black pepper. Season the second tray of flour with more kosher salt and plenty of cayenne and paprika. This is the main heat component of the chicken, so use your head here: If you like it spicy, use about 6 tablespoons cayenne. Doctor this according to your tastes. Paprika isn't hot, and it's mostly there for aroma and color; 4 tablespoons is what I used.

4. Working with one piece of chicken at a time, shake the excess marinade off and then drag it through the first tray of flour, coating it on both sides. Shake off the excess, then drag it through the buttermilk, coating both sides, and shaking off the excess again. Finally, drag the chicken through the spicy flour, coating both sides, but don't shake off the excess. Transfer to a plate and repeat with the remaining chicken.

5. Fry the chicken in batches by gently lowering it into the hot oil and letting it cook for about 7 minutes, making sure to turn it occasionally to cook the meat evenly—it'll be dark reddish brown. If using a Dutch oven, adjust the heat to keep the oil at 375°F, as the chicken will cause the oil to drop in temperature. Remove the chicken from the fryer and allow to drain and rest on a paper towel–lined plate or a wire rack set over a tray to catch the oil. Season with just a little more kosher salt. Reserve 2 tablespoons of the oil.

TO MAKE THE SAUCE:

6. While the chicken is resting, combining all the sauce ingredients in a medium bowl. Pour this mixture into a medium saucepan and heat on medium-low until the onions are tender.

TO MAKE THE BOWL:

7. Add the reserved oil from frying to a nonstick pan and fry the eggs over medium heat to your preferred level of doneness.

8. Divide the rice between two serving bowls. Place the chicken on top of the rice, then drizzle the sauce over the top. Top each bowl with a cooked egg. If you'd like, you can use a food coloring marker to draw a star on the oblate discs to match Cable's eye, then use the discs to garnish the eggs. Add pickles, and devour in good company!

Runaways Okonomiyaki

Teams often include some of my favorite Marvel characters, and the teen team of the Runaways is no exception. It can be tough sometimes to represent all of the characters through food, but I knew an okonomiyaki (it means "cooked how you like it" in Japanese) would be a great vessel for our adolescent allies, so feel free to riff on the toppings to create your own super team of savory pancake goodness. If you check out the *Eat the Universe* video in which I make this recipe, I noted that the character Nico Minoru is represented by the magical mucilage contained in *yamaimo*, a Japanese mountain yam. If you can't find yamaimo or nagaimo (another type of mountain yam), blanched and grated okra has a similar texture. I haven't tried using a regular russet potato, but I'm sure that would also work. I also strongly advise you use Japanese mayo rather than regular mayo—I have the logo of my favorite Japanese mayo (Kewpie) tattooed on me because it's *that* good.

PANCAKE BATTER:
One 2-inch-long yamaimo or nagaimo yam (or russet potato), grated
2 eggs
1 teaspoon mirin
½ cup water
1 cup all-purpose flour
1 teaspoon baking powder
2 teaspoons hondashi (dashi powder) or chicken bouillon
1 pound kale
Juice of ½ lemon
½ cup cooked, shredded chicken

NOODLES:
2 tablespoons vegetable oil
1 portion (5 ounces) fresh yakisoba noodles
1 tablespoon okonomiyaki sauce or steak sauce

TOPPINGS:
Aonori (seaweed flakes)
Katsuobushi (bonito flakes)
Japanese mayonnaise or regular mayonnaise
Okonomiyaki sauce

TO MAKE THE PANCAKE BATTER:

1. In a small bowl, combine together the yam, eggs, mirin, and water. Then, in a medium bowl, combine together the flour, baking powder, and hondashi or chicken bouillon.

2. De-rib the kale by removing the tough stems and tearing the leaves into pieces. I personally think it's very fun to do, so maybe you can task a kid with this step. Put the leaves in a large bowl with the lemon juice. Rub and squeeze the kale until it is coated with lemon juice and the color brightens.

3. Add the wet works into the dry works while stirring. Add the kale and shredded chicken and stir once more to combine.

TO MAKE THE PANCAKE:

4. In a large pan over medium-high heat, add the vegetable oil. Once the oil is hot, about 2 minutes, add the yakisoba noodles and okonomiyaki sauce and toss to cook the noodles. It's okay if a few get stuck to the pan.

5. Corral the noodles into a circle and pour the pancake batter over the top. Let the batter cook about 4 to 5 minutes without disturbing it. You might see some bubbling happen on the surface. Carefully—and I mean it—use the biggest spatula you have to flip the pancake. Hesitation will cost you here, so flip it quickly and firmly. Leave the pancake on the heat until the batter is cooked through, about 4 to 5 more minutes. You can test this with a chopstick or toothpick by inserting it into the middle of the pancake. If it comes out with liquid batter stuck on it, the pancake needs to keep cooking.

6. Once the pancake is cooked, top it how you'd like with dashes of the seaweed and bonito flakes, a few drizzles of mayonnaise and okonomiyaki sauce, then devour!

Rocket Raccoon's Trash Omelette

Poor Rocket Raccoon, the trash panda of the Marvel Universe, is one of my favorite characters. I love his scrappiness! And this is a dish you can make using scraps! I happened to have a leftover chicken carcass and Indian food and I came up with this recipe. If you don't have these specific leftovers lying around, make like the robots that crafted Rocket and experiment! I bet Rocket would blast me for that joke. Just like Rocket has an affinity for the explosive, this dish packs a punch and will wallop any breakfast or dinner hunger pangs. It's a riff on *omurice*, a Japanese dish that I'd wager was invented to use up extra rice. If you don't have any leftovers, this dish works fine with fresh-made white rice, though it won't have the same saucy punch. This recipe includes directions for making chicken stock, which is a great way to use up leftovers, but you can also use store-bought stock as well.

TIP: Some other vegetable trimmings you can include in your stock are mushroom stems, carrot tops, the woody ends of asparagus, corn cobs, potato parings, herb stems, and more. You'll have a good amount of stock left over from this recipe. Feel free to add some salt and pepper and use it as a base for your next soup.

Cooked chicken carcass
Stems and leaves of 3 to 5 beets, separated
3 to 5 onion skins
1 bunch cilantro
¼ cup plus 2 tablespoons vegetable oil, divided
1 tablespoon olive oil
Kosher salt
Black pepper
½ lemon
2 cups leftover cooked rice (we used rice and chicken tikka masala)
4 eggs
2 tablespoons unsalted butter
1 to 3 ketchup packets, or 1 ounce ketchup

TO MAKE THE STOCK:

1. In a large stock pot, cover the chicken carcass with cold water, add the beet stems (reserving the leaves for later), onion skins, and any other vegetable trimmings you may have lying around and bring to a boil. Cook for about 1 hour or until the stock has developed a nice aroma. Strain, discard the vegetable trimmings, and set the stock aside.

TO MAKE THE GREENS AND RICE:

2. Meanwhile, in a blender pulverize the cilantro and ¼ cup of the vegetable oil until it is liquefied. Strain this mixture through two coffee filters set in a colander or sieve over a glass bowl. This might take some time, but the good news is that the flavored oil will keep, refrigerated, for weeks (unlike fresh cilantro).

3. Take the beet leaves you separated out earlier, roll them up, and slice into strips. Toss them in a medium bowl with the olive oil and salt and pepper to taste. Use a rasp grater to zest the lemon half onto the dressed greens and toss to incorporate.

4. Heat the remaining 2 tablespoons vegetable oil over medium-high heat in a medium pan. Add the leftover rice and cook until toasted, stirring frequently. Add the leftover Indian food and stir until warmed and cooked through.

TO ASSEMBLE:

5. In a medium bowl, beat the eggs together with 2 ounces (about ¼ cup) of the chicken stock you made. Season with salt and pepper.

6. In a nonstick pan over medium-low heat, melt the butter and cook until foamy.

7. Add the eggs and allow to cook for about 30 seconds. Stir the eggs twice using a rubber spatula, then cover and cook for about 2 more minutes. Check the eggs and spread any uncooked portion to the edge of the omelette. Cover and cook 1 minute more.

8. Slide the omelette into a medium bowl—try not to tear it, and try to keep the omelette open—then fill the bowl with the fried rice mixture. Place a plate over the bowl and invert to make a rice-filled omelette dome of goodness.

9. Put the ketchup in a small bowl and add a few tablespoons of the chicken stock, then stir to loosen up the ketchup to a pourable consistency. Drizzle onto the omelette. Top with the dressed beet leaves and cilantro oil and devour.

10. "I am Groot."

Deadpool's Chimichangitas

If Deadpool is the "Merc with a Mouth," does that also mean he's known for his palate? Secret fact: Deadpool doesn't really love chimichangas; he just loves saying the word. Well, Deadpool has never had my chimichangitas, which are tiny chimichangas that are so delicious you will break the fourth wall and possibly mutter a &^%#! or two. Chimichangas are basically deep-fried burritos, but you can get away with shallow-frying these little nuggets of nom, or, if you're the kind of person who has an air fryer, just spritz them with oil and air-fry until golden brown.

Four (10-inch) flour tortillas
¼ cup all-purpose flour
¼ cup water
1 cup shredded sharp cheddar cheese
½ cup cooked black beans, drained
1 cup cooked white rice
1 cup finely shredded cooked chicken
Canola oil for frying
Kosher salt
Red enchilada sauce, warm, for garnishing
Mexican crema for garnishing
Sliced black olives for garnishing

1. Using a 4-inch ring cutter, cut 3 small tortillas from each large tortilla. Wrap the small tortillas in a damp paper towel and microwave until pliable, about 10 seconds.

2. In a small bowl, combine the flour and water and mix until smooth.

3. Arrange the small tortillas on a clean work surface. Leaving a ½-inch border around the outer edge, assemble cheese, black beans, rice, and chicken in the center of each tortilla, taking care not to overfill.

4. Roll each filled tortilla into a chimichangita by folding two opposite sides slightly over the filling, then folding the bottom edge entirely over the filling. Spread a small layer of the flour-water mixture over the top edge and roll the tortilla into a chimichangita. The flour-water mixture will help it stay sealed.

5. Fill a large skillet with 1 inch of canola oil and place over medium heat. To test if the oil is ready, drop a small piece of leftover tortilla into the oil; it should bubble immediately. Remove the test piece of tortilla and carefully put the chimichangitas in. If the pan is looking crowded, fry the chimichangitas in batches. Cook, turning occasionally, until deeply golden brown on all sides, about 8 minutes total. Reserve the fried chimichangitas on a wire rack set over a lined baking sheet. Season with salt to taste.

6. Arrange the warm chimichangitas in a plastic food basket or on a platter and add a liberal amount of enchilada sauce. Drizzle with crema and scatter with black olives.

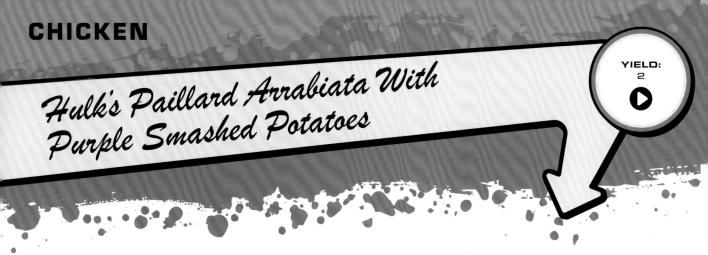

Hulk's Paillard Arrabiata With Purple Smashed Potatoes

YIELD: 2

Hulk does what Hulk does best in this dish—*smash! Arrabiata* means "angry" in Italian, but unlike Bruce Banner, you *will* like this sauce when it's angry. I wanted to represent the iconic green-and-purple color scheme that Hulk is famous for, so I used purple potatoes. They're becoming popular in grocery stores, but if you can't find them substitute some red potatoes and give a nod to Thunderbolt Ross, the Red Hulk.

Two 6-ounce boneless, skinless chicken breasts
1 cup all-purpose flour
3 eggs, beaten
1 cup Italian bread crumbs
Kosher salt
1 pound small purple potatoes, boiled
Canola oil
½ yellow onion, diced
1 jalapeno, minced
2 cloves garlic, minced
Pinch of red pepper flakes
½ cup white wine
2 cups packed fresh parsley leaves
8 cups packed baby spinach
2 tablespoons unsalted butter
Juice of 1 lemon

1. Cut the chicken breasts in half horizontally to form 4 thin cutlets. Sandwich the chicken cutlets in a single layer between two large pieces of plastic wrap. Pound to about ¼ inch thick.

2. Arrange 3 shallow dishes or trays and place the all-purpose flour in the first, the beaten eggs in the second, and the Italian breadcrumbs in the third. Season the flour with salt. Dredge the chicken cutlets in the flour, then the eggs, and finally the bread crumbs, shaking off any excess after each step. Place the dredged cutlets on a plate and set aside.

3. Place the boiled potatoes between two dinner plates. Firmly press down to smash until about ½ inch thick.

4. Place a sauté pan over medium heat and add enough canola oil to coat the bottom of the pan.

5. Add the onion and cook until slightly softened, about 5 minutes. Add the jalapeno, garlic, and red pepper flakes and cook until aromatic, about 3 minutes. Add the white wine and scrape up any brown bits that may have accumulated. Add the parsley and spinach and cook until wilted, about 3 minutes. Add the butter and stir to combine.

6. Transfer the cooked vegetable mixture to a blender and blend until smooth. Add the lemon juice and salt, to taste, and pulse to combine.

7. Wipe the sauté pan clean and add about ¼ inch of canola oil. Place over medium-high heat.

8. Working in batches if necessary, fry the chicken cutlets until deep golden brown and cooked through, about 5 minutes per side. Set the cooked chicken on a paper towel–lined plate.

9. Still working in batches if necessary, add the smashed potatoes to the pan and cook until the edges are crispy, about 3 minutes per side. Season with salt and set aside with the chicken.

10. To serve, arrange the potatoes and chicken on a small plate and cover the chicken in green sauce.

BEEF

The Punisher's Italian Wedding Soup

YIELD:
4
▶

Francis Castiglione, Frank Castle, or The Punisher—whatever you call him, you know he's on a mission of vengeance and vigilante justice. In some runs of the comic, he learns his military might in the Vietnam War. I wanted to bring both his Italian and Vietnamese influences to this recipe, so what we have is an Italian wedding soup flavored like pho, and the results are punishingly delicious. If you don't want to make your own broth, just use store-bought beef broth.

If you don't have a pressure cooker, it's no big deal. Simply follow the instructions, but allow the broth to simmer in a stock pot for about three hours first. Then follow the directions from the point of pressure release.

BROTH:
3 pounds halved marrow bones, or any beef bones, split
1 onion, split
1-inch knob fresh ginger, halved
4 cloves garlic, smashed
1 stick cinnamon
5 whole cloves
3 pods cardamom
20 black peppercorns
4 pods star anise
Kosher salt, for punishing

MEATBALLS:
½ pound ground beef
½ pound ground pork
2 tablespoons fresh minced parsley
2 tablespoons fresh minced basil
½ cup grated Parmesan cheese
¼ cup Italian bread crumbs (or panko or homemadebread crumbs)
1 egg
Kosher salt, for punishing
Ground black pepper, also for punishing

EGG STRACCIATELLA:
2 eggs
¼ cup grated Parmesan cheese
1 head escarole, torn

TO MAKE THE BROTH:

1. Combine all of the broth ingredients including salt to taste in a pressure cooker and fill with water until everything is covered. Lock the lid on the pressure cooker, set to high pressure, and cook for 15 minutes once pressure is reached.

TO MAKE THE MEATBALLS:

2. While the broth cooks, in a large bowl combine all meatball ingredients with a tender touch. The more you mash, the tougher the meatballs. Season the mixture with plenty of salt and pepper—maybe just a little more than you think. If you need a measurement, try 2 teaspoons salt and 1 teaspoon pepper.

3. Roll into 1-inch balls and refrigerate until it's time to finish the soup.

TO MAKE THE EGG STRACCIATELLA:

4. In a small bowl, beat the eggs, then stir in the cheese. Refrigerate until you are ready to finish the soup.

TO ASSEMBLE:

5. Once the broth has cooked, carefully strain out the veggies, spices, and bones. Any little bits of meat or marrow stuck to the bones are good to eat with a little salt and make a fine mini-boss reward, because you are about halfway done with this recipe.

6. Once the broth is strained, transfer to a container to cool. Once it is cool, a hard layer of fat will form on top. I like a fair amount of fat in my soup, but you can scrape it all off and add back as much as you like once the soup is hot.

7. Reheat the broth to a boil, then add the meatballs one by one. Once the broth again returns to a boil, punish it with more salt and pepper to taste. Finish by adding the escarole and then slowly drizzling the egg mixture in while stirring. Serve immediately with a side of revenge.

Moon Knight's Chicago Dog Pizza

YIELD: 1

Is this pizza masquerading as a Chicago dog or a Chicago dog masquerading as pizza? Whatever its true identity, it's delicious. Moon Knight has many alter egos that he uses to get crime-fighting information, so I thought this taste bud–confusing dish would be appropriate for him. Moon Knight's Chicago origins are heavily channeled in this team-up of New York–style pizza and a Chicago dog, modeled after his frequent partnership with our favorite web-head. And you shouldn't have trouble finding neon green relish (seriously, that's what it's called), a common Chicago dog topping.

1 pound prepared pizza dough
All-purpose flour, for dusting
3 all-beef hot dogs, sliced into rounds to resemble pepperoni
1 white onion, diced, divided
Sport peppers in brine
2 plum tomatoes, cut into wedges, divided
Dill pickle spears, sliced, brine reserved
½ cup yellow mustard
Olive oil for brushing
1 teaspoon poppy seeds
8 ounces part-skim mozzarella, shredded
Neon green relish for serving
Celery salt for serving

1. Preheat the oven to 500°F.

2. Dust a work surface with a light coating of flour, then toss, roll, shape, or stretch the pizza dough into a 16-inch round. If you want to toss it, I suggest making a fist and tossing the dough back and forth from fist to fist to naturally stretch it out. Then lay it down on the floured work surface and use your fingers to continue stretching the dough to the right size. No method is particularly right or wrong. Just make it thin and round, with a lip, aka a crust, on it. Transfer to a pizza pan and set aside.

3. In a medium sauté pan over medium heat, add the hot dog slices and fry until crisp, about 8 minutes. Use a slotted spoon to transfer them to a paper towel–lined plate.

4. In the same pan, still over medium heat, add half the onion and sauté until softened, about 4 minutes. Add about ¼ cup of the sport pepper brine liquid and scrape up any brown bits that may have accumulated in the pan. Add a few sport peppers, to taste, half the tomatoes, about ¼ cup pickle brine, and the yellow mustard. Bring to a simmer and cook until thickened slightly, about 2 minutes.

5. Carefully transfer the mixture to a blender and blend until smooth to make your pizza sauce.

6. Brush the pizza dough with olive oil, sprinkle with poppy seeds, and add a layer of your new sauce. Sprinkle with the mozzarella cheese and top with the remaining onion, tomatoes, sliced pickles, and hot dogs. Bake until the cheese is melted and the crust is browned and crisp, about 20 minutes. Top with neon green relish and sprinkle with celery salt before cutting and serving on a paper plate. For maximum effect, fold the pizza in half and eat while walking to your nearest public transit hub.

Captain America Beef Tongue Terrine

YIELD: 2

Steve Rogers, Captain America, the man out of time, probably loved beef tongue when he was young. See, back then people ate cheaper cuts of meat to help the war effort. He also grew up in a tenement during the Depression. But here's a secret: Beef tongue is absolutely delicious and as close to a beef-based Super-Soldier Serum as I'll get. You can find beef tongue at many international markets or butcher shops. You'll also need two clean and empty tin cans for this recipe. This dish is a nod to Cap's roots, to patriotism, and to, well, just making do with what you have to support a bigger belief.

1 beef tongue, about 2½ to 3 pounds
½ cup cold water, plus more as needed for braising
2 tablespoons coarsely chopped parsley
Zest of 1 lemon
Three ¼-ounce gelatin packets
Kosher salt
Yellow mustard for serving

1. Preheat the oven to 275°F.
2. Place the raw beef tongue in a Dutch oven. Fill with water to cover halfway. Cover with lid and place in oven. Cook for 6 hours. Let the entire vessel cool at room temperature. Once cool, reserve the braising liquid, then use a sharp knife to peel the skin from the tongue. Discard the skin and cube the remaining meat.
3. Place cubed tongue in a large bowl and combine with parsley and lemon zest.
4. Pour 1½ cups of the braising liquid into a medium pot and bring to a simmer. In a medium heatproof bowl, add the packets of gelatin to the ½ cup of cold water and whisk to dissolve. Add the hot braising liquid to the gelatin mixture and stir to combine. Season with salt to taste.
5. Divide the tongue mixture evenly between the two clean, empty soup cans, then carefully pour the gelatin mixture into both cans so the meat is fully covered.
6. Transfer the cans to the refrigerator and chill until solid. This could take some time depending on how full your fridge is, but 6 hours should do the trick.
7. Remove from the fridge, and use a can opener to open the bottom of the cans. Run an offset spatula or butter knife around the inside of the can to release the aspic.
8. Push out your gorgeous tongue baby, slice, plate, and serve with yellow mustard.

Uncanned X-Men Loco Moco

On this episode of *Eat the Universe*, I challenged myself to make a dish out of canned ingredients, which are generally seen as, well, rather canny. My guests on that episode were there to talk about the X-Men, so I wanted to show off *my* mutant power: the ability to make a dish out of practically anything. What resulted was a loco moco made mostly of canned ingredients. Just call me the Professor X of flavor.

One 12-ounce can ham
Freshly ground black pepper
8 ounces cooked bacon
1 cup canned corn, drained
1 cup canned mixed peas and carrots, drained
1 dried shiitake mushroom cap
½ cup water
One 13.5-ounce can coconut milk
½ cup chocolate-hazelnut spread
2 tablespoons soy sauce
¼ large red bell pepper, seeded and ribs removed
4 eggs
Coarsely chopped cilantro for serving
Zest of 1 lemon for serving
Kosher salt

1. On the largest holes of a box grater, grate the canned ham. Form into 4 patties and season with black pepper. Set aside.

2. Place a large skillet over medium heat and add the bacon. Cook until the bacon is warm and about 2 tablespoons of fat have rendered, about 7 minutes. Transfer the bacon to a plate lined with paper towels and leave the fat in the pan. Add the corn, peas, and carrots to the pan and sauté until golden brown, about 5 minutes. Transfer to a bowl and set aside. Increase the heat to high and add the ham patties to the pan. Sear until crisp, about 5 minutes per side, and transfer to a plate. Coarsely chop the bacon and set aside.

3. Combine the mushroom cap and water in a small heatproof bowl. Microwave for 5 minutes on medium power to make a mushroom broth. Be careful removing the bowl from the microwave; it will be hot. Remove the mushroom from the bowl and coarsely chop. Reserve the broth.

4. In a medium saucepan, combine the mushroom broth, chopped mushroom, coconut milk, chocolate-hazelnut spread, soy sauce, and black pepper to taste. Whisk to combine, and place over medium heat. Char the red bell pepper directly over a gas burner, turning regularly so the exterior is evenly charred and the interior is soft, about 5 minutes. Slice the pepper and add to the coconut milk mixture. Simmer the mixture until thickened slightly, about 10 minutes. Strain and keep warm.

5. In a large nonstick skillet, fry the eggs to your desired doneness.

6. To serve, place a ham patty on a plate. Top with sautéed vegetables and an egg. Finish with the coconut milk gravy, chopped bacon, cilantro, and lemon zest.

Angel's Meatloaf Wellington

YIELD:
1
▶

You might have to ask a grandparent about Angel, one of the very first Marvel characters, created way back in 1939 (as opposed to Warren Worthington III of the X-Men). Interestingly, this Angel—also known as Thomas Halloway—appeared in Marvel Comics #1, which was actually printed by Timely Comics, the predecessor to Marvel Comics as we know it.

You don't have to be a great detective like Angel to know that meatloaf can be less than super. But just like Thomas Halloway, who didn't have any superpowers, all it takes to make something super is dressing it up in the right garb. In the case of meatloaf? Puff pastry. This dish is still "timely" even today and is a fun take on the weeknight classic.

3 eggs, divided
1 pound ground chuck
1 pound ground pork
½ cup plain bread crumbs
1 yellow onion, minced
2 cloves garlic, minced
1 teaspoon kosher salt
1 tablespoon water
1 sheet puff pastry, halved and thawed
½ cup all-purpose flour
Chopped chives for garnishing

1. Preheat the oven to 350°F.

2. In a large bowl, lightly beat 2 of the eggs. Add the ground chuck, ground pork, bread crumbs, onion, garlic, and salt. Using your hands, fold the mixture together until incorporated. Transfer to a standard 9-by-5-inch loaf pan and bake the loaf at 350°F until just cooked through, about 1 hour. Let cool at room temperature, then transfer to the refrigerator until completely chilled.

3. Once the meatloaf has chilled, preheat the oven to 425°F.

4. In a small bowl, combine the remaining 1 egg with the tablespoon of water to create an egg wash, then set it aside.

5. Roll each piece of puff pastry to approximately 11 by 7 inches, using the flour to dust the board and rolling pin to keep the pastry from sticking if necessary. Line a small baking sheet with a silicone baking mat or parchment paper. Wrap the meatloaf by placing the first piece of puff pastry on the baking sheet and the chilled meatloaf on top of it, centered. Then lay the second piece of puff pastry over the meatloaf, covering it completely. Trim the edges of the pastry if necessary. Crimp the edges to fully enclose, then liberally coat with the egg wash. Using a sharp knife, cut several slits in the top to allow steam to escape.

6. Bake until puffed and golden brown, about 30 minutes. Garnish with chives and serve warm.

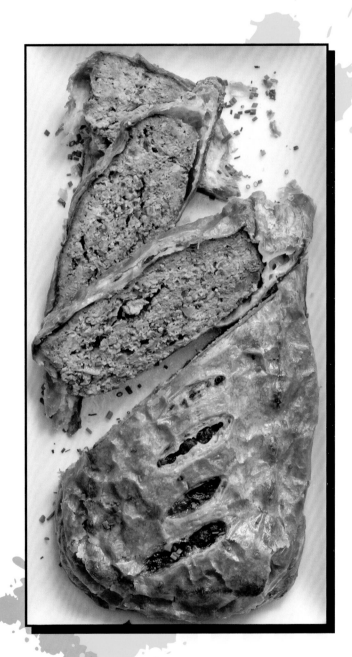

Storm's Tournedos of Beef

YIELD: 2

I mean, come on, when the dish is called "tournedos" in reference to the filets, who in the Marvel Universe do *you* think of? Storm controls the weather, so in this dish we make clouds of whipping cream and you can make it rain truffles if you've got them. No truffles? Snag some truffle oil, now available in most supermarkets, and, well, make it drizzle. And the numbing effect of the Szechuan peppercorns will provide an electrifying tingle on your tongue. To represent Storm's stint in X-Men Gold, we've got some golden polenta in place of the croutons used in the classic tournedos Rossini. This recipe also calls for goose or duck liver, and though they're an important component of the dish they can easily be omitted if you don't have access to them.

Two 8-ounce filet mignons
2 cups heavy whipping cream
Kosher salt
½ teaspoon ras el hanout
2 medallions goose or duck liver, sliced 1 inch thick
Ground black pepper
2 slices precooked packaged polenta, sliced about 1 inch thick
1 teaspoon Szechuan peppercorns
1 cup dry red wine
1 tablespoon pregelatinized or instant flour
Finishing salt, such as fleur de sel, for garnishing
Shaved fresh black truffle or truffle oil for garnishing

1. Allow the filet mignons to come to room temperature.

2. In the bowl of a stand mixer, combine the heavy whipping cream, a pinch of salt, and the ras el hanout and beat on high until stiff peaks form. You can also do this in a large bowl with a hand mixer. Set aside.

3. Place a large cast-iron skillet over medium-high heat. Place the livers in the pan and sear until deeply golden brown, about 5 minutes per side. Leave the fat in the pan and transfer the livers to a cooling rack set over a baking sheet.

4. Season the filets with salt and pepper. In the same pan you cooked the livers in, sear to medium-rare, about 4 minutes per side over medium-high heat.

5. Transfer the filets to the cooling rack with the livers. Add the polenta to the pan and sear until golden brown, about 2 minutes per side. Transfer to the cooling rack with the livers and filets.

6. Add the peppercorns to the pan and toast, stirring frequently, until very fragrant, about 2 minutes. Add the red wine and then carefully ignite the sauce by gently touching the flame from a long-handled lighter to the liquid. Flames will flare up quickly as the alcohol is burned off. After the flames subside, simmer the wine mixture to reduce slightly, about 2 minutes.

7. Add the flour to the wine mixture and stir to combine. Simmer to thicken, about 2 more minutes, and season with salt.

8. To serve, spoon the sauce onto plates. Place a filet in the middle of each plate, then stack the polenta and liver on top of the filet. Garnish with the savory whipped cream, finishing salt, and shaved black truffle or a drizzle of truffle oil.

Thor's Meat Mjolnir

Thor without his hammer is like steak without a bone. It's just not super. Here we use a tomahawk steak to mimic the might of Mjolnir in a feast suitable for any Asgardian upon ascending to Valhalla. To further increase the Norse influence in this dish, I add creamed fish roe to the mashed potatoes. These can be found in tubes online (they don't spoil!) or at your favorite Swedish flat-packed furniture store (wink). Although fish eggs in potatoes may sound like I fell off the Bifrost, they are actually a great complement, providing some salt and a little bit of funk—something I'd bet the Asgardians of the Galaxy could get behind. I'd give my right eye to eat some right now.

1½ pounds Yukon gold potatoes, quartered
Kosher salt
1 tomahawk steak, brought to room temperature
Canola oil
Freshly ground black pepper
½ cup heavy cream, warmed
¼ cup (½ stick) unsalted butter, at room temperature
¼ cup creamed fish roe

1. Preheat the oven to 400°F. Place the potatoes in a large pot. Cover with water to a height of 2 inches above the top of the potatoes, season with salt, and place over high heat. Bring to a boil and cook until tender, about 25 minutes.

2. While the potatoes are boiling, preheat a grill pan over medium-high heat, flat-side up. Pat the steak dry with paper towels.

3. Liberally season the steak with canola oil, salt, and pepper. Place the steak on the grill pan and sear until deeply golden brown, about 6 minutes. Flip the steak and transfer it, still on the grill pan, into the oven for about 10 minutes to finish cooking to desired doneness. Use a meat thermometer to check the temperature. The steak's internal temperature should reach 125°F for medium-rare and 135°F for medium. Let rest at room temperature for about 10 minutes before slicing.

4. Drain the potatoes, then add them back to the dry pot. Add the cream, butter, and creamed fish roe and mash to desired consistency.

5. Serve the potatoes hot alongside the steak.

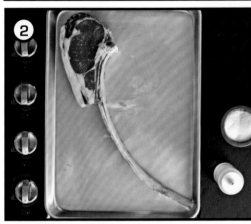

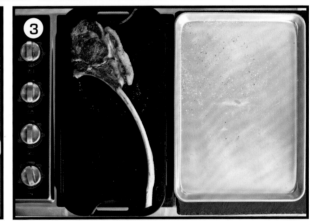

FOR ASGAAAARD!

PORK

Golden Oldie Eggs Benedict

YIELD:
1

Aunt May is probably one of the best-known mother figures in the Marvel Universe, having raised Peter Parker from an early age. Aunt May was also briefly a herald of Galactus when she assumed the title of Golden Oldie. This dish will eat perfectly fine without the gold leaf and is a great way to show the super-mother figure (or anyone who likes to eat) in your life that you care. And guess what? Hollandaise is one of the five "mother sauces" of French cooking.

3 egg yolks
Pinch of kosher salt
Juice of 1 lemon (about 2 tablespoons)
¾ cup (1½ sticks) unsalted butter, melted
5 sheets gold leaf (optional)
1 English muffin, split and toasted
2 slices Canadian bacon
2 poached eggs

1. In a blender, combine the egg yolks, salt, and lemon juice. Pulse to combine.
2. Working a few tablespoons at a time, add the melted butter and blend well between each addition.
3. Add the gold leaf, if using, and pulse several times to incorporate.
4. To serve, place the English muffin on a plate, cut sides up. Top with the Canadian bacon, poached eggs, and a generous portion of the golden hollandaise sauce. Serve warm.

Juggernaut's Breakfast Burrito

YIELD: 1 LARGE OR 2 SMALL

Juggernaut is one big dude, and when he's not charging through walls and X-Men I bet Cain Marko has one heck of an appetite. If you've seen this episode of *Eat the Universe*, you know I go to great lengths to craft the largest tortilla I can—and you can do the same, providing you have a big enough space to cook it on. Chances are a pizza stone or big frying pan will be your best bets. I used a giant paella pan to get the job done. For fillings, I used cooked hot bacon, refried beans, chopped ham, chorizo, scrambled eggs, apples, cheese, peppers, onions, and hash browns. No matter how good you feel after eating this, please do not charge through a wall.

2 cups all-purpose flour, plus more for dusting
1½ teaspoons baking powder
1½ teaspoons kosher salt
3 tablespoons lard or cold bacon grease
¾ cup warm water
Burrito fillings

1. Stir together the 2 cups of flour, baking powder, and salt in a large bowl. Rub the lard or cold bacon grease into the dry ingredients until the dough begins to look like cornmeal. Add the warm water and stir to combine until all of the water has been absorbed.

2. Flour a work surface and knead the dough on it a couple of times. Sprinkle a little more flour on the work surface and roll out the dough into a giant tortilla shape, roughly 20 inches in diameter. Or you can create two smaller tortillas instead.

3. This is where it gets tricky. To make the giant tortilla, I used a paella pan and a pot boiler propane burner, but I recognize that most people won't have these things lying around. You can achieve similar if smaller results by dividing the tortilla dough in two and cooking each half on a preheated pizza pan or pizza stone in an oven at 350°F. Regardless, cook briefly, about 90 seconds per side, until the dough is cooked but still pliable.

4. Fill the tortilla with exciting pre-cooked breakfast burrito ingredients, then carefully roll everything up by first folding in the sides and then rolling the entire burrito. Finally, devour the burrito.

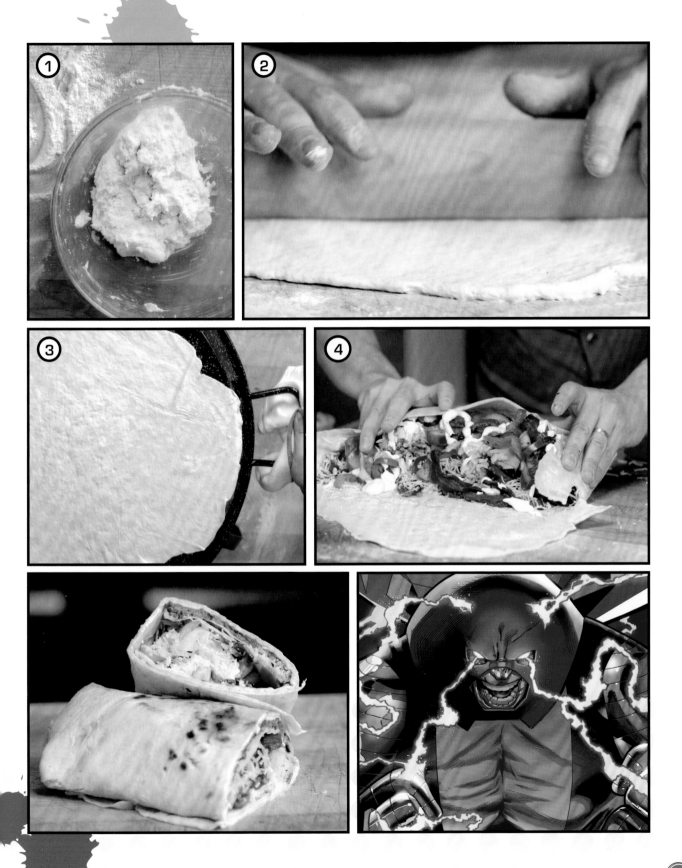

Ghost-Spider's Bodega Sandwich

YIELD: 1

Ghost-Spider literally rocks. She's easily one of my favorite Spider-People. I love the details in the Marvel Universe: You see, in New York City, corner stores, convenience stores—whatever you want to call them—are called "bodegas." And as one of the Forgettable Foes of Ghost-Spider, Bodega Bandit has a special place in my hipster heart. Bodegas often have a menu of items that can be ordered from the griddle, and the king of them is the bodega sandwich, which is at a minimum two eggs on a roll and at a maximum whatever you desire.

1 round bread roll, halved horizontally
2 tablespoons mayonnaise
½ pound bacon strips
3 eggs
Kosher salt
Black pepper
2 slices pepper jack cheese
Ketchup for serving
Pickled jalapeños for serving

1. Place a large nonstick skillet over medium-high heat. Liberally spread both cut sides of the roll with mayonnaise. Toast cut side down until golden brown, about 5 minutes. Set aside.

2. Keeping the skillet over medium-high heat, add the bacon and cook until crisp, about 10 minutes. Transfer to a paper towel–lined plate, leaving the bacon fat in the skillet.

3. Crack the eggs into a medium bowl and whisk lightly. Season with salt and pepper. Reduce the heat to medium-low and add the eggs to the skillet with the bacon fat and stir until slightly set. While the top of the scrambled egg is still a bit loose, add the pepper jack cheese. Fold the egg over itself to envelope the cheese and finish cooking. Fold the egg again so it is a quarter circle and transfer it to the bottom half of the toasted bun.

4. Garnish as desired with ketchup and pickled jalapenos. Cut in half and serve.

Loki's Kroppkakor

YIELD: 12

Just like Loki, kroppkakor are a surprise wrapped in mystery. These Swedish dumplings look like little potatoes on the outside; after all, they're made of potatoes. But on the inside lies the real excitement—a sweet bacon and onion filling. I love serving these guys as a side dish, as they can be filled with any number of fillings. I bet this recipe's ability to shapeshift would make the god of mischief smile.

10 medium white potatoes, peeled, boiled, and cooled
1 egg, beaten
1½ cups all-purpose flour, divided, plus more for dusting
8 ounces raw bacon, diced
1 medium yellow onion, finely diced
1 teaspoon ground allspice
Kosher salt
Lingonberry jam, for serving
Sour cream, for serving

1. In a large bowl or pot, use a potato masher or ricer to mash the potatoes.

2. Add the beaten egg and 1¼ cups of the flour to the potatoes and stir until smooth. If the potatoes are looking a little thin, add the additional ¼ cup of flour. Set aside.

3. Set a medium sauté pan or skillet over medium-low heat. Add the diced bacon and the onion to the pan and cook until the onion is soft and the bacon is beginning to brown, about 8 minutes.

4. Add the allspice to the onion and bacon mixture and continue to cook for 1 minute or until aromatic, then set aside to cool.

5. Using floured hands and a clean work surface, shape the potato mixture into a log and cut into 12 pieces. Flatten each piece into a disk and use your thumb to create a well in the center of each one.

6. Place 1 tablespoon of the bacon and onion mixture, drained, on each potato disk, then fold up the sides and crimp with your fingers while shaping into a ball.

7. Bring a large pot of water to a boil, add about 1 tablespoon of kosher salt, and boil the balls in batches, about 6 at a time, until they float, about 7 minutes.

8. Keep in a warm place, covered with plastic wrap, until ready to serve. Serve with lingonberry jam and sour cream.

Triathlon's '90s Pulled Pork

Anything you can do, Triathlon can do three times faster. With the help of a pressure cooker, the same applies to your kitchen. Triathlon first appeared in the '90s, so I wanted to make a super-'90s presentation for this dish. This style of plating was copied by many chefs in the '90s, just like the Triune Understanding copied 3-D Man's powers and bestowed them to Delroy Garrett, creating Triathlon. If you don't have a pressure cooker, give Triathlon a day off and use a slow cooker according to the manufacturer's instructions.

One 4-pound boneless pork shoulder
1 cup water, beef stock, or root beer
Kosher salt
Prepared barbecue sauce
Prepared mashed potatoes
Prepared collard greens

1. Place the pork shoulder and the water, stock, or root beer in a pressure cooker. Lock the lid, set to high pressure, and place over medium heat. Once pressure has been reached, allow the pork to cook for 1 hour before quick-releasing the valve.

2. Allow the pork to cool a bit before shredding with two forks or gloved hands. Season with kosher salt.

3. To serve, use a squeeze bottle to draw a circle of barbecue sauce around the perimeter of a plate. Use a ring mold in the center of the plate to construct a tower: mashed potatoes on the bottom, followed by the collard greens and then the pork. Remove the ring mold and marvel at the '90s presentation.

Hercules's Pork Souvlaki

A lot of Marvel heroes borrow from mythology—I'm looking at you, Thor—and Hercules is based upon Heracles of Greek mythology. Hercules is known for doing strong-guy stuff, and with the doing of strong-guy stuff, you're gonna need some calories. For this I recommend a herculean portion of souvlaki, which is marinated meat on a stick. And you can wash it down with a serving of Thena's Cold Energy Feta Frozen Yogurt (page 124).

1½ pounds pork tenderloin, cut into bite-sized pieces
½ cup extra-virgin olive oil
Juice of 2 lemons
2 tablespoons red wine vinegar
2 tablespoons chopped fresh oregano
1 tablespoon chopped fresh thyme
2 cloves garlic, minced
1½ teaspoons kosher salt
1 teaspoon black pepper
Tzatziki sauce for serving
Sliced cucumbers for serving
Pita bread for serving

1. Soak 6 bamboo skewers in a shallow pan full of water. Make sure the skewers are completely submerged.

2. Meanwhile, combine all the ingredients except the tzatziki, cucumbers, and pita in a bowl until uniform and the pork is coated. Cover with plastic wrap and refrigerate overnight or at least 3 hours.

3. After the pork has marinated, preheat a grill or grill pan over medium-high heat. Thread the pork chunks onto the bamboo skewers, then grill, turning every 3 minutes until slightly charred and cooked through, about 10 minutes total.

4. Serve with tzatziki sauce, cucumbers, and pita.

Black Panther's Akabenzi

Black Panther is the king of the secretive East African country of Wakanda, a Vibranium-powered land of awesomeness. I've been fortunate enough to visit this area of Earth-616, and one of the best things I got to eat was *akabenzi*, a fried pork dish that has as much kick as T'Challa's Vibranium-enhanced suit. *Akabanga*, the hot sauce that supercharges this dish, can be found online, or you can substitute your favorite hot sauce. If you can't find shiso to make your heart-shaped herb, you can trim basil leaves into similar shapes.

¼ cup ketchup
¼ cup Dijon mustard
1 tablespoon lime juice
1 tablespoon soy sauce
¼ cup honey
2 ounces ginger, peeled and minced
2 ounces garlic, peeled and minced
1 teaspoon Akabanga or other hot sauce
1 rack pork back ribs (roughly 1 to 1½ pounds)
2 cups water
2 limes
1 shiso leaf

1. Combine the ketchup, mustard, lime juice, soy sauce, honey, ginger, garlic, and hot sauce in a large bowl. Slice the ribs apart and toss them in the marinade. Cover, then refrigerate overnight.

2. Once the ribs have finished marinating and you're ready to cook, preheat the oven to 250°F. Place the ribs in a large Dutch oven and add the water. Reserve the marinade. Cook, covered, for 3½ hours.

3. When the ribs are done baking and the meat is tender, use a spoon to skim some pork fat from the Dutch oven. Add about 2 to 3 tablespoons of this fat to a large frying pan over medium-high heat. Pan-fry the ribs in the fat until they have browned a bit. Plate the ribs in a deep serving dish.

4. Create a sauce by combining the cooking liquid in the frying pan with the leftover marinade. Cook over medium-high heat until the sauce comes to a boil. Pour the sauce over the ribs. Halve the limes and add to the top of the dish so your guests can squeeze some fresh juice on their serving if they would like. Top with a heart-shaped shiso leaf, and serve a dish fit for a king.

SEAFOOD

The Great Video's Deconstructed Tuna Noodle Casserole

YIELD:
8

Heathrow Vance was given X-ray powers by an experiment gone explodey. He turned to a life of crime as the Great Video, putting on stage shows while scanning the pockets of his audience for his henchmen to later rob. He was the baddie du jour in *Marvel Boy #1* way back in 1950, an era when things were simpler and a staple dish was tuna noodle casserole. Here we use our "x-ray vision" to find the deliciousness within the original dish and repurpose it into swirly "eyes" of evil. Don't look too long or . . . well, I guess you'll have to read *Marvel Boy #1*.

PEA PUREE:
5 ounces fresh or frozen peas (defrosted)
1 to 2 tablespoons heavy cream
Kosher salt
Freshly ground black pepper

BÉCHAMEL SAUCE:
2 tablespoons butter
2 tablespoons all-purpose flour
1 cup milk
Kosher salt
Freshly ground black pepper

DECONSTRUCTED CASSEROLE:
4 cooked and cooled lasagna noodles
1 sushi-grade tuna fillet (about 4 to 6 ounces), seared quickly on all sides

TO MAKE THE PEA PUREE:

1. Combine the peas with the heavy cream and a pinch of salt and pepper in a food processor or blender. Blend until smooth, then set aside.

TO MAKE THE BÉCHAMEL SAUCE:

2. Add the butter to a small saucepan over medium-low heat and melt. Whisk in the flour until well combined.

3. Add the milk and whisk continuously until the sauce is smooth and has thickened, about 2 minutes. Season with salt and pepper.

TO ASSEMBLE:

4. Start by using your X-ray vision to stare through a tuna noodle casserole to see its component parts. Flatten the noodles and add a smear of béchamel sauce to each one.

5. Slice the fillet into 4 slices, then slice them again down the middle, lengthwise. Using a dish or a pan, press the tuna into even thinner slices.

6. Place the flattened tuna atop the sauced noodle, and add a dollop of pea puree on the end nearest you.

7. Beginning with the end with the puree, roll the noodle tightly, then cut in half. Repeat with the remaining noodles.

8. Serve with the frilly ends facing up, like a pair of creepy X-ray eyes.

Nebula's Salmagundi

YIELD:
4

Nebula is a space pirate—possibly the raddest career of all. Pirate food is generally whatever you can plunder, but historians agree that salmagundi, a hodgepodge of fish, fruit, and shelf-stable ingredients, is an actual dish that actual pirates ate. Although none of the ingredients are particularly cosmic, your guests will certainly think you've visited other galaxies when they see the wild presentation of totally edible and delicious fish skeletons. If you don't have a century egg available, just use two hard-boiled eggs. Additionally, if you'd rather not make ceviche shrimp, you can use precooked shrimp and marinate it with the same dressing.

1 pound shrimp, peeled and deveined
7 limes, divided
Kosher salt
1 cup cilantro leaves
¼ cup extra-virgin olive oil, plus more to taste
1 hard-boiled egg, peeled and halved lengthwise
1 century egg, peeled and halved lengthwise
1 mango, cut, peeled or unpeeled
Pinch of red pepper flakes
4 sardines, scaled and deboned
1 cup green olives, pitted
1 cup black oil-cured olives, pitted
1 cup toasted pecans
1 cup shelled pistachios, toasted
One 14-ounce can whole hearts of palm, quartered lengthwise
One 15-ounce jar sliced pickled beets
2 cups green seedless grapes
2 cups purple seedless grapes
1 lemon, sliced

1. Halve the shrimp lengthwise and add to a bowl. Add the juice of 2 limes and a pinch of kosher salt, to taste. Let the shrimp marinate in the lime juice until opaque, about 20 minutes. The lime juice will "cook" the shrimp.

2. In a blender, combine the juice of 4 limes and the cilantro. Blend until smooth. While the blender is running, slowly drizzle about ¼ cup extra-virgin olive oil to make an emulsified dressing. Season with salt.

3. When the shrimp has finished marinating, toss it with the cilantro dressing.

4. Season the eggs with salt and pepper. Season the mango with red pepper flakes. You can slice it and serve it unpeeled as I have, or you can cut the cubes off the skin for easier eating. Slice the remaining lime.

5. Drizzle the sardines and olives with olive oil.

6. On a large plate or platter, assemble all of the components by laying them down around the platter in sections, placing the marinated shrimp on top. Finish with a squeeze of lemon across the platter, along with a drizzle of any leftover dressing. Serve immediately.

Shang-Chi's Salt and Pepper Squid Rings

YIELD: 2

If you're a real Marvel fan, you know that Shang-Chi's enemy, the Mandarin, wields ten rings that he got from an alien race known as the Makluan. Although I don't have access to alien technology, some would argue that squid are some of the most alien-looking creatures we eat. And guess what? You can turn them into delicious golden-fried rings. Here, in a nod to Shang-Chi's Chinese roots, I give the squid a simple treatment of salt and pepper, one of my favorite preparations found in Cantonese restaurants.

Vegetable oil for frying
2 pounds large squid, cleaned and sliced into rings
1 tablespoon Chinese cooking wine or mirin
1 teaspoon sesame oil
½ cup all-purpose flour
½ cup yellow cornmeal
2 teaspoons kosher salt, plus more for seasoning
1 teaspoon white pepper, plus more for seasoning

1. Fill a Dutch oven with about 2 inches of oil, or fill a deep fryer according to manufacturer's instructions. Preheat to 350°F.

2. In a large bowl, combine the squid, Chinese cooking wine or mirin, and sesame oil.

3. Combine the flour, cornmeal, salt, and pepper in a medium bowl.

4. Once the oil is hot, dredge the squid in the flour mixture and add to the oil, working in batches to maintain the oil temperature.

5. Cook until golden, about 3 minutes, then drain on paper towels.

6. Taste a squid ring, and adjust the seasoning as needed.

Iron Man's Lobster Corn Dog

For this episode of *Eat the Universe*, I was challenged to make a snack that Tony Stark, the invincible Iron Man, would eat at a sports game. I came up with this, the lobster corn dog. Like Iron Man, lobsters too have a red shell. And you have to have the wealth of Tony Stark if you want to eat them all the time. To further "bouge-out" this baller dish, we add caviar and gold leaf, while leavening with champagne. If you don't have a wallet like Tony Stark's, use cheap lumpfish caviar, edible gold luster dust (available online), and leaven with whatever yummy bubbly liquid you have, such as a sparkling wine or cider of your choice.

Canola oil, for frying
1 cup Japanese mayonnaise
Juice of 1 lemon
1 ounce black sturgeon caviar
Two 1½-pound whole cooked lobsters
1⅓ cups finely ground cornmeal
2 cups all-purpose flour, divided
1 teaspoon sugar
1 teaspoon baking powder
¼ teaspoon baking soda
¾ cup buttermilk
½ cup creamed corn
½ cup champagne
Kosher salt
Gold leaf for serving

1. Fill a deep fryer according to the manufacturer's instructions and preheat to 375°F. Alternately, you can fill a Dutch oven or other heavy-bottom pot halfway full with oil and heat to 375°F over medium heat.

2. In a quart-size zip-top bag, combine the mayonnaise, lemon juice, and caviar. Massage the bag to mix the ingredients, and set aside.

3. Tear the tails from the bodies of the lobsters. Using kitchen shears, carefully cut down the shell of each tail and remove the meat. Discard the shells. Thread a wooden chopstick or thick skewer halfway through each piece of tail meat to create a handle for your corndog. Using a spoon, scoop the tomalley (the digestive gland of a lobster) from the body of each lobster and add to a large bowl. Reserve remaining lobster meat for another use of your choice.

4. To the bowl with the tomalleys, add the cornmeal, 1 cup of the flour, the sugar, baking powder, and baking soda and stir to combine. Add the buttermilk, creamed corn, and champagne and whisk to combine to create a batter.

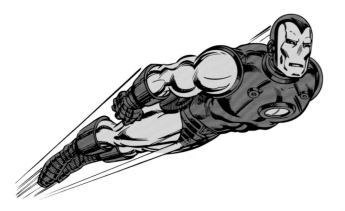

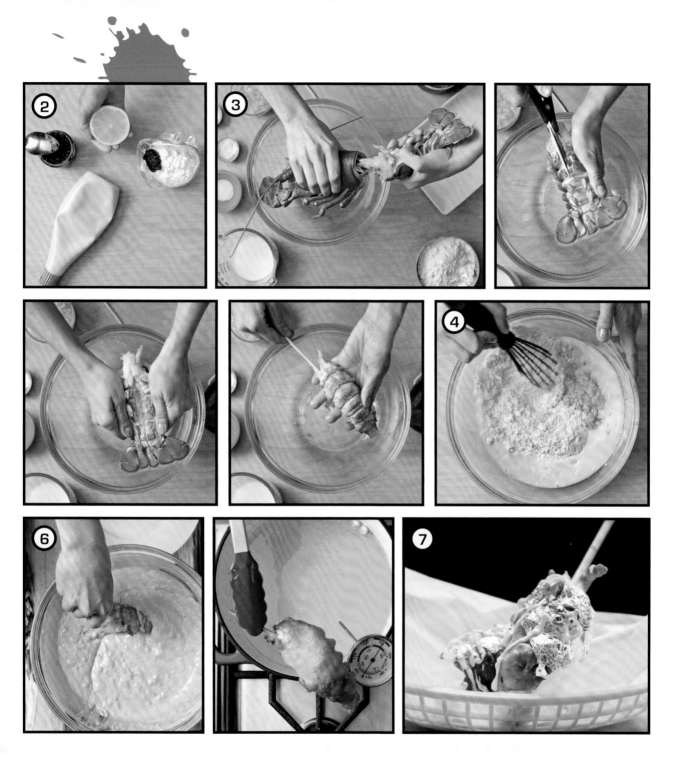

5. Place the remaining 1 cup flour in a shallow dish.

6. Holding the handle of a corndog, dredge the lobster tail in the flour and shake off any excess. Dip in the wet batter next, shake off any excess, and, still holding the handle of the corndog, carefully dip in the fryer oil. Make sure the whole corndog is immersed in the oil and cook, holding it, until crisp and deep golden brown, about 3 minutes. You might want to wear an oven mitt to keep your hand safe from the heat and oil. After frying, rest the corndogs on a paper towel–lined plate and season with salt to taste.

7. Top with gold leaf (if using) and the caviar mayonnaise and serve hot.

Silver Surfer's Clam Tacos

There are few instances of the Silver Surfer eating. After all, he's imbued with the Power Cosmic, granting Norrin Radd all sorts of powers, but mostly the ability to be silver, surf the cosmos, and not be hungry. Is not being hungry a power? I like eating so much it would be a curse to me. Anyway, at one point, the Silver Surfer ends up in New England, where he kinda sorta falls for a local—and they eat what I would assume to be clam chowder. I thought making the surfer favorite of seafood tacos, but filled with what you'd find in classic New England clam chowder, would be a real win for this Marvel hero. If you can't find silver leaf, silver luster dust is more common. You can always wrap the tacos in aluminum foil before serving, but unless you have the Power Cosmic, don't eat the foil itself!

Canola oil for frying
2 tablespoons unsalted butter
1 russet potato, peeled and diced
1 yellow onion, thinly sliced
1 carrot, julienned
3 celery heart ribs, thinly sliced
Juice of 4 limes
Kosher salt
1 cup sour cream
2 tablespoons clam juice
1 cup all-purpose flour
Black pepper
1 pound Manila clams, shelled, juices reserved
4 corn tortillas
Silver spray (optional)
Silver leaf (optional)

1. Place a large heavy pot or Dutch oven over medium-high heat and fill with 2 inches canola oil. Preheat to 375°F.

2. While the oil is heating, place a large skillet over medium-high heat. Add the butter, and when the butter bubbling subsides, add the diced potatoes. Cook the potatoes, tossing occasionally, until the outsides are golden brown and the insides are tender, about 8 minutes.

3. In a large bowl, toss the onions, carrots, and celery with the lime juice and a generous pinch of salt. Set aside.

4. Combine the sour cream and clam juice in a zip-top bag. Stir to create a crema. You can transfer this to a squeeze bottle or create one yourself by simply cutting the tip off a bottom corner of the bag when you're ready to dispense.

5. Once the canola oil has reached 375°F, pour the flour into a shallow dish and season liberally with salt and pepper. Dredge the clams in the flour.

6. Working in batches, fry the clams until they're golden brown, only about 2 minutes, then place them on a paper towel-lined plate to rest. Make sure the oil returns to 375°F between each batch.

7. Toast the tortillas briefly on a warm, dry skillet, then spray them with silver spray, if using.

8. To serve, place the crema, clams, potatoes, and vegetables on the middle of a tortilla, then top with silver leaf, if using. Fold and enjoy!

Fritto Misto Sub-Mariner Sandwiches

YIELD: 2

Namor, the Sub-Mariner. This recipe practically writes itself. The king of Atlantis would assuredly approve of this ocean-sourced monster of food, all packed onto a sub (see what I did there!?) and slathered with some yummy fish sauce–enhanced dressing and the salad of the sea: seaweed.

Canola oil, for frying

1 pound mixed seafood, cleaned, such as bay scallops, shrimp, calamari, oysters, or white fish

4 cups all-purpose flour, divided

1 cup pregelatinized or instant flour

2 cups seltzer water

Kosher salt

Freshly ground black pepper

½ cup Japanese mayonnaise

2 tablespoons rice vinegar

1 teaspoon fish sauce

2 tablespoons sambal chile sauce

1 tablespoon soy sauce

Pinch of sugar

Fresh seaweed

Parsley leaves for serving

Cilantro leaves for serving

2 submarine sandwich rolls, split horizontally

1. Fill a large deep fryer according to the manufacturer's instructions and preheat to 375°F. Alternately, you can fill a heavy-bottom pot such as a Dutch oven halfway with oil and heat to 375°F over medium-high heat.

2. Cut calamari into ½-inch rings, oysters into 1-inch pieces, and fish into ½-inch pieces.

3. In a large bowl, combine 2 cups of the all-purpose flour and the instant flour. Add the seltzer water and stir to combine to create a the wet batter. Put the remaining 2 cups all-purpose flour in a shallow dish. Season both the all-purpose flour and the wet batter with a generous amount of salt and pepper.

4. Dredge a few pieces of fish in the flour, shake off any excess, then dip in the wet batter, coating it completely. Carefully lower the fish into the fryer and fry until deeply golden brown, about 3 minutes. Transfer to a paper towel–lined plate and season with salt. Repeat the process with the remaining seafood. Be sure not to fry too many pieces at once or the temperature of the oil will drop.

5. In a small bowl, combine the mayonnaise, rice wine vinegar, fish sauce, chile sauce, soy sauce, and sugar. Whisk to combine.

6. Add the seaweed, mayonnaise sauce, and fresh herbs to either cut side of the rolls, then mound with fried seafood. Top with the other half of the roll and serve warm.

Rogue and Gambit's Red Beans and Rice

Though Gambit might be the ragin' Cajun, his *chérie,* Rogue, is assuredly also familiar with this Southern classic, growing up as she did in Mississippi. Just like Mr. and Mrs. X, the team of red beans and rice is a true marriage, making a complete protein upon digestion and generally bringing out the best in each other. What I love most about red beans and rice is that independently they are side dishes, but together they become a meal. And that, my friends, is one heck of a team-up.

This recipe calls for dried epazote, a leafy herb common in Mexican cuisine. You can find it in international markets.

1 pound dried kidney beans
3 bay leaves, divided
2 white onions, peeled; 1 halved, 1 diced
1 tablespoon canola oil
1 green bell pepper, seeded and ribs removed, diced
2 ribs celery, diced
3 tablespoons dried epazote leaves
2 cloves garlic, minced
3 pieces tuna jerky, about 2–3 inches long
2 fillets smoked trout, about 8 ounces total
1 tablespoon fish sauce
Cajun seasoning
Cooked white rice for serving

1. Soak the dried beans overnight in enough water to cover them by 2 inches.

2. Pour the water and soaked beans into a large stockpot and add 1 of the bay leaves and the halved onion. Bring to a boil, then reduce to a simmer and cook until tender, about 1 hour. Set aside to cool completely, then drain, reserving both the beans and the cooking liquid.

3. In a large Dutch oven over medium-high heat, add the canola oil followed by the diced onion, bell pepper, and celery. Sauté until the onion is slightly translucent, about 7 minutes. Add the epazote, garlic, remaining 2 bay leaves, tuna jerky, and smoked trout. Stir to combine, then add the fish sauce and a dash or two of Cajun seasoning, to taste. Continue to cook until the vegetables begin to caramelize, about 10 minutes. Add the reserved bean liquid and scrape any brown bits that may have accumulated in the bottom of the pot. Reduce the heat to low.

4. Add the kidney beans and mash slightly with a potato masher. To serve, portion the cooked rice into bowls and top with kidney beans.

Wolverine's Bayou Boil

YIELD: 4

I made this to celebrate Wolverine's adventures around New Orleans in *Wolverine: The Lost Trail*. There's something super fun about making claw kebabs—especially when they are skewered components of a bayou boil! Crawfish, just like Wolverine, have a healing factor—they can regenerate their limbs—and yes, they have claws! If you don't have access to crawfish (they are pretty easy to find frozen online, and possibly in the frozen section of big grocery stores), shrimp will also transport your taste buds to the Big Easy.

Two 3-ounce pouches crab boil seasoning in a bag
1 pound medium red potatoes
2 ears corn, husks and silks removed and cut into thirds
8 ounces andouille sausage, cut into ½-inch rounds
1 pound frozen whole crawfish, thawed
Juice of 1 lemon
Kosher salt

1. Fill a very large stock pot halfway with water and bring to a simmer. Add the crab boil pouches and simmer until the water is heavily seasoned, about 5 minutes.

2. Add the potatoes and cook until tender, about 15 minutes. Remove with a slotted spoon and set aside. Add the corn and cook until tender, about 5 minutes. Remove with a slotted spoon and set aside.

3. Thread the potatoes, corn, sausage, and crawfish onto 12-inch metal skewers. Season the crawfish boil water with the lemon juice and salt to taste. Submerge the skewers, handle up, in the simmering water and cook until the crawfish are bright red and cooked through, about 5 minutes.

4. Serve on butcher paper or newspaper and eat with your hands, pulling pieces off the skewers and enjoying.

Wilson White Fisk With Blood Orange Sauce

YIELD: 2

The Kingpin of crime has always been one of my favorite characters. I'm fascinated by his ability to craft elegant schemes to further his agenda, while still having brute force to back him up should things unravel. If you've seen the video for this recipe, you know there are a bunch of Daredevil-ish ingredients in this dish, from hojicha "Stick" tea to avocados (at law). But what I like most is that it's just like the Kingpin—elegantly composed, but still packs a punch. Xanthan gum is an emulsifier and can be found at specialty food stores or online. And remember, if you can't cook in Hell's Kitchen, any kitchen will do.

1 pound (4 sticks) plus 2 tablespoons unsalted butter
1 pound cod or other firm white fish, cut into 2 fillets
¼ cup water
Pinch of xanthan gum
1 tablespoon hojicha green tea
1 tablespoon sugar
2 teaspoons red pepper flakes, plus more for garnishing
1 cup blood orange juice
2 teaspoons kosher salt, plus more for finishing
1 avocado, sliced
Ground black pepper

1. In a tall pot, melt the pound of butter over medium-low heat. Once the butter is melted, carefully add the cod and cook until tender and flaky, about 10 minutes.

2. While the fish is poaching, place a medium saucepan over medium heat and add the water and the remaining 2 tablespoons butter. Add the xanthan gum, hojicha, sugar, and red pepper flakes and cook until the butter is melted and the sauce is simmering. Strain this liquid into a large bowl with the blood orange juice and whisk until combined. Season to taste with kosher salt.

3. Divide the sauce among serving plates, then add a fillet of fish to the center of each plate. Top with sliced avocado, black pepper, salt, and additional crushed red pepper flakes.

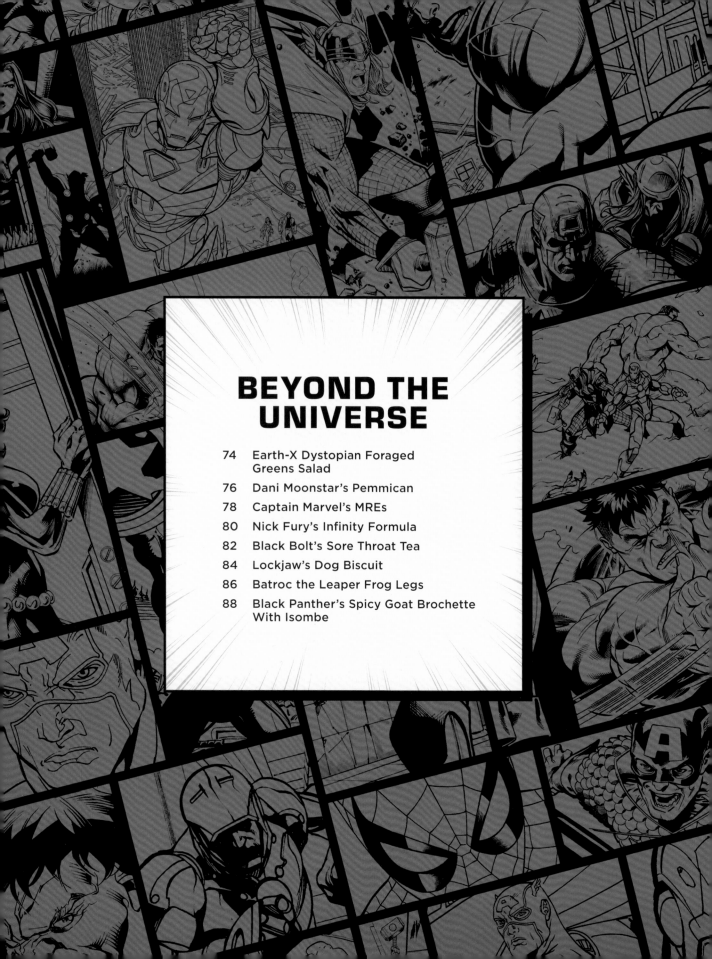

BEYOND THE UNIVERSE

Earth-X Dystopian Foraged Greens Salad

YIELD: 1 LARGE ▶

Earth-X is a dystopian version of Earth (Earth-9997 to be specific), a place where everyone has superpowers. This leads to, well, dystopia. And when life gives you dystopia, you gotta make do with what you can scavenge. In this case, it's wild plants, mushrooms, bugs, and things that don't go bad. If you are hesitant to eat bugs (you shouldn't be—they're delicious, and you can find them online), just omit them from the recipe to make a delightful salad. You can get sea beans online, or you can just swap them out for green beans.

½ cup canola oil, plus more for frying, divided
2 sunchokes, thinly sliced
Kosher salt
8 ounces oyster mushrooms, broken into 2-inch pieces
2 cups dandelion greens, cut into 1-inch strips
¼ cup kimchi, coarsely chopped
¼ cup kimchi liquid
2 cups watercress, divided
⅓ cup sea beans
Silkworm pupa, cleaned and roasted (optional)
Black ants, cleaned and roasted (optional)
Wasps, cleaned and roasted (optional)
Grasshoppers, cleaned and roasted (optional)

1. Place a large skillet over medium-high heat and pour in a generous amount of canola oil so it covers the bottom of the pan.

2. When the oil is hot, add the sunchokes and cook until crisp and golden brown, flipping once halfway through cooking, about 4 minutes each side. Transfer to a paper towel–lined plate, season with salt to taste, and set aside.

3. Add another thin layer of canola oil to the pan if necessary and add the mushrooms. Cook until deeply golden brown, tossing occasionally, about 7 to 10 minutes. Season with salt to taste. Add the dandelion greens and kimchi to the pan and reduce the heat to low.

4. Pour the kimchi liquid into a small bowl. Drizzle in the ½ cup canola oil, whisking continuously. Add to the skillet, scraping up any brown bits that may have accumulated. Add 1 cup of the watercress along with the sea beans, silkworm pupa, ants, wasps, and grasshoppers, if using.

5. Garnish with the remaining 1 cup watercress. Serve warm.

Dani Moonstar's Pemmican

YIELD:
8

I'll never forget reading The New Mutants in my teens. It was the perfect time for the perfect comic book. I connected to Dani Moonstar's plight as an adolescent, and it didn't hurt that my uncle lived in her home state of Colorado. Thanks to *Eat the Universe*, I got to reconnect with the character as an adult chef. Pemmican is the original protein bar—as long as it's kept moderately cool, it stays good for a long time and is packed with nutrients to keep you pumped while projecting psionic illusions of your enemies' greatest fears.

3 pounds bison sirloin steak
Kosher salt
8 ounces beef suet
½ cup dried cherries
½ cup toasted sunflower seeds
Collard leaves, uncooked, for serving
Honey for serving

1. Line oven racks with extra wide aluminum foil and preheat to the lowest setting.

2. Slice the bison against the grain into thin strips. Lay the strips in a single layer on the foil-lined oven rack and season with kosher salt to taste.

3. Place the racks in the oven and stick a wooden spoon in the oven door to crack slightly to allow moisture to escape. Dehydrate the bison until it is the consistency of beef jerky and no moisture remains, about 6 to 8 hours.

4. Place the beef suet in a small pot over medium heat. Stirring occasionally, melt until completely liquid and golden. If any bits remain, pour through a fine-mesh sieve and discard. Keep warm until ready to use.

5. Place the dehydrated bison in a food processor and pulverize until the largest pieces are about ¼ inch. Transfer the bison to a bowl. Add the cherries to the food processor and pulse to coarsely chop. Add the sunflower seeds and pulse a few more times. Add the cherries and sunflower seeds to the bison. Season with salt to taste and stir to combine.

6. Add about ¼ cup melted beef suet to the bison mixture and stir to combine. This should be enough suet to hold the mixture together when firmly pressed. If not, add more suet a tablespoon at a time until the mixture holds together.

7. Lay a collard green leaf on a clean work surface and transfer about ½ cup pemmican mixture onto the center. Firmly press into a bar, wrap with the collard leaf, and tie with kitchen twine.

8. To serve, unwrap the collard green and drizzle the pemmican with honey. Serve at room temperature.

Captain Marvel's MREs

YIELD: 6

Most MREs—or meals ready to eat—are a bunch of precooked vacuum-sealed, uh, "food." Even a Skrull wouldn't want to mimic what comes in our soldiers' and astronauts' pouches. For this recipe, I thought I'd make the original MRE: canned goods. This is a basic recipe for canning that I'd wager Carol Danvers could have seen in action during her summers in Maine. You'll need to use proper canning equipment and techniques to ensure everything is sterilized.

4 pounds beef stew meat, cubed
1 tablespoon salt
1 teaspoon black pepper
2 tablespoons vegetable oil
10 medium potatoes, peeled and cubed
5 carrots, peeled and sliced
4 celery ribs, chopped
3 onions, diced
1 teaspoon fresh thyme
2 bay leaves
1 tablespoon soy sauce
1 tablespoon Worcestershire sauce

1. In a pressure canner, heat 6 quart-sized mason jars in simmering water.
2. Season the meat with the salt and pepper.
3. Add the oil to a large pot over medium-high heat. Once the oil is shimmering, add the meat and increase heat to high, turning the meat occasionally to brown the exterior, about 6 minutes.
4. Add the remaining ingredients to the pot, cover with water, and bring to a boil.
5. Once the mixture is at a boil, carefully ladle the stew into the jars, leaving 1 inch of space at the top. Wipe the rims of the jars and apply the lids and bands until they are just secured on the jars.
6. Cook the jars in the pressure canner for 1½ hours. Then turn off the heat and allow the pressure to come down naturally. Once the pressure is totally released, allow the jars to cool and check the seals the following day. If the seals are intact, the meals will keep for quite a while.
7. To serve, open a mason jar, add the stew to a pot, and bring to a boil.

Nick Fury's Infinity Formula

If work is what you are looking to do, this meal-replacement Infinity Formula smoothie will get the job done. Nick Fury has certainly had to put in some overtime, and I don't think most restaurants deliver to Helicarriers (yet). The chia seeds and maca powder in this recipe can be found at health food stores or online. You can also add alternative flavorings, but be advised it will change the caloric content.

2 cups grapefruit juice
1 cup frozen berries
1 banana
2 teaspoons chia seeds
1 teaspoon maca powder

1. Combine all ingredients in a blender and blend until smooth.

Black Bolt's Sore Throat Tea

Black Bolt can decimate an opponent just by uttering one word using his quasi-sonic scream. That's gotta do a number on one's throat, Terrigen Mist exposure or not. Here I used black tea and ginger, which both have anti-inflammatory properties, to make this sore-throat-soothing beverage.

1 black tea bag
Honey
Pinch of kosher salt
Lemon wedge
1 teaspoon grated fresh ginger

1. Add all ingredients to a mug that makes you laugh or feel better in any way. Top with boiling water and steep for 6 minutes before removing the tea bag.

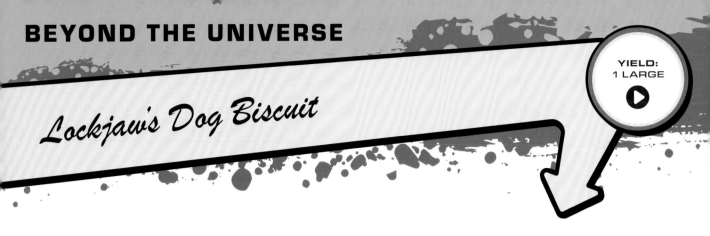

Lockjaw's Dog Biscuit

**YIELD:
1 LARGE**

Lockjaw is my favorite dog in the Marvel Universe, and I absolutely adore my dog too, so I thought it would be fun to make a recipe in honor of this teleporting hound. Don't worry, it's safe for humans to eat too, although the flavor is pretty mild so as not to irritate any puppy tummies.If my dog had Lockjaw's powers, I'm sure we'd teleport to her favorite place on Earth-616: the fuzzy blanket on my couch.

3 cups whole wheat flour, plus more for dusting
1 teaspoon kosher salt
2 large eggs
½ cup canned pumpkin puree (not pie filling)
¼ cup creamy peanut butter
1 cup water or as needed

1. Preheat the oven to 350°F. Grease a sheet pan and line it with parchment paper.

2. Combine all the ingredients except the water in the bowl of a stand mixer using a paddle attachment on low speed. Once fully combined, add water until the dough comes together into a shaggy mass.

3. Flour a clean work surface, along with your hands. Scoop out the dough and knead it 10 to 15 times or until it is no longer sticky.

4. Use a loaf pan, rolling pin, or other flat surface to press or roll the dough until it's about ¾ inch thick, then form it into an elongated dog bone–shaped biscuit. You can also shape the dough into multiple smaller dog bone-shaped biscuits for dogs smaller than Lockjaw. Transfer to the prepared lined sheet pan.

5. Bake for about 1 hour or until hardened. Let cool before serving to your favorite super pup, such as Lucky the Pizza dog, Thori, Rambo, Sassafras, Cerberus, Ms. Lion, Deuce, or Dogpool.

Batroc the Leaper Frog Legs

YIELD:
1

Batroc, or Batroc the Leaper, is a French dude with a serious ability to jump and kick. That might not sound like much, but he definitely annoys the heck out of Captain America on more than a few occasions. In celebration of both his French and amphibian origins, this recipe is for frog legs. Frog legs taste like something between white fish and chicken, so if you don't have access to frog, by all means use either as a substitute. If you can get frog, you will jump for joy at how delicious this turns out.

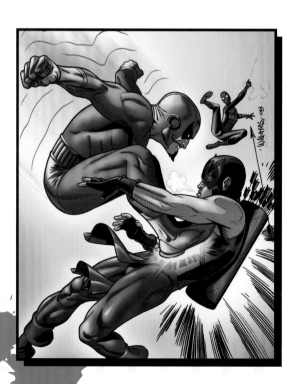

1 cup all-purpose flour
Kosher salt
4 tablespoons unsalted butter, divided
3 pairs frog legs
1 shallot, finely diced
1 cup white wine
Juice of ½ lemon
Parsley sprig for garnishing

1. Preheat the oven to 350°F.

2. Pour the flour into a shallow dish and season with salt. Place a nonstick skillet over medium-high heat and add 2 tablespoons of the butter. When the butter foam subsides, dredge the frog legs in the flour, shake off the excess, and add to the pan. Sear until golden brown, about 4 minutes per side. Transfer the legs to a small baking sheet lined with a cooling rack. Bake in the oven until the legs are cooked through, about 8 minutes.

3. While the frog legs are in the oven, return the pan to the stove, still over medium-high heat, and add the remaining 2 tablespoons butter. Once melted, add the shallot and season with salt. Whisk to combine and cook until translucent, about 3 minutes. Add the white wine and lemon juice, bring to a simmer, and cook to reduce slightly, about 3 minutes.

4. To serve, arrange the frog legs on a plate. Strain the sauce through a mesh sieve and spoon it into the bottom of the plate. Garnish with a single sprig of parsley and enjoy.

Black Panther's Spicy Goat Brochette With Isombe

YIELD: 2

Brochette is just a simple grilled meat on a stick, and isombe is like creamed spinach—but with peanut butter! I had both dishes while hanging out in East Africa, and I can imagine Shuri and T'Challa fighting over the last brochette while Okoye snags it in the end. If you're nervous about cooking goat, which is more commonly eaten in a lot of countries outside the United States, substitute lamb, pork, or beef. It'll still be fit for a king!

Shito is a Ghanaian pepper sauce and can be found in some international markets, along with the cassava leaves.

ISOMBE:
Kosher salt
1 small eggplant, peeled and chopped
3 tablespoons palm oil
1 white onion, chopped
1 green bell pepper, seeded and chopped
2 cups cassava leaves, chopped fine
1 cup water
½ cup smooth peanut butter

BROCHETTES:
Kosher salt
1½ pounds goat shank meat, cubed
Oil for brushing on the grill
Shito sauce

TO MAKE THE ISOMBE:

1. Salt the eggplant and let it sit for at least ½ an hour or up to 1½ hours to draw moisture from the eggplant. Squeeze the liquid from the eggplant, discarding the liquid and setting aside the eggplant.

2. Place a large skillet over medium heat. Add the palm oil, then the onion and sauté for about 2 minutes. Add the bell pepper and sauté about 2 more minutes, then add the eggplant and sauté about 2 minutes longer. Add the cassava leaves and the water.

3. Reduce the heat to low and simmer until the cassava leaves are tender, roughly 30 minutes. In the meantime, you can make the brochettes. To finish the isombe, stir in the peanut butter, season with salt to taste.

TO MAKE THE BROCHETTES:

4. Soak 4 wooden skewers in water for ten minutes to prevent them from scorching.

5. Season the skewers with salt and thread the meat onto them.

6. Rub oil on grill grates and heat the grill over high heat in a well-ventilated area. Once the grill is hot, place the skewers on the grill, rotating frequently. Once the brochettes are getting good grill marks, brush them on all sides with the shito sauce.

7. Once the goat has reached an internal temperature of 145°F, take the brochettes off the heat and plate them beside the finished isombe, then devour them with your Vibranium claws.

VEGETARIAN

Adam Warlock's Eggs in Cocoon

YIELD: 4

Adam Warlock gets resurrected multiple times in the Marvel Universe, and emerges from a cocoon in doing so. This lends itself to a nice play on words for this version of the French dish *oeufs en cocotte*, in which eggs are cocooned in a covered baking dish. After all, a breakfast of an egg in a thick tomato stew is something I'd definitely want to eat after being annihilated and brought back by cosmic regeneration. Toast is an ideal accompaniment to this dish!

Extra-virgin olive oil
½ medium yellow onion, chopped
1 clove garlic, minced
One 28-ounce can crushed tomatoes
4 large eggs
1 ounce crumbled Edam cheese (or another cheese of your choosing)
Kosher salt
Black pepper

1. Preheat the oven to 350°F.

2. Place a medium pot over medium heat and add about 2 tablespoons olive oil.

3. Once the oil is shimmering, add the onion and cook until softened, about 5 minutes, then add the garlic and continue to cook about 2 more minutes. Add the tomatoes and cook until slightly reduced, about 6 minutes.

4. Rub 4 ramekins with olive oil and add some tomato mixture to each, enough to cover the bottom by about ½ inch. Add 1 egg to each ramekin, then top each egg with cheese and salt and pepper to taste.

5. Prepare a water bath by pouring about ½ inch of hot water into a baking dish. Evenly space the ramekins in the baking dish and bake until just set, 12 to 15 minutes.

6. Remove the baking dish from the oven. Carefully remove the ramekins from the hot water and allow to cool slightly before serving.

Doctor Strange's Agamotto Pickle Spheres

YIELD: 4

You don't have to live at 177A Bleecker Street to get some of the wildest ingredients in the cosmos. There are plenty of online retailers who will happily deliver things like xanthan gum and sodium alginate to you even if your house is not the Sanctum Sanctorum. These orbs (or eyes, or spheres) of green brine make an ideal amuse-bouche for any supremely sorcerer-ific soiree. The texture might not be ideal for the faint of heart, but neither is the madness of the Dark Dimension. This recipe is measured in grams because the proportions need to be exact; use a kitchen scale.

200 grams pickle brine, plus more for storage
0.75 gram xanthan gum
2 grams calcium lactate
1500 grams water
7.5 grams sodium alginate

1. In a high-speed blender, combine the pickle brine, xanthan gum, and calcium lactate. Blend on high speed until thoroughly mixed, about 1 minute. Transfer the mixture to a container, cover, and refrigerate overnight.

2. Rinse out the blender and dry thoroughly. Combine the water and sodium alginate in the blender and blend on high speed until thoroughly combined, about 3 minutes. Transfer the mixture to a container, cover, and refrigerate overnight.

3. Once the pickle mixture is chilled, pour it into a squeeze bottle and set aside while you prepare the sodium alginate bath. If using silicone molds, fill the molds with the pickle mixture and freeze at least 3 hours.

4. Transfer the sodium alginate bath to a microwave-safe container and microwave on high for 4 minutes or until just warmed.

5. Dribble the pickle mixture into the warmed alginate bath to create "caviar" or "pearls." If using silicone molds, remove each frozen pickle cube from the mold and place in the alginate bath, making sure they don't touch. Use a spoon to gently drizzle the alginate bath over the frozen pickle liquid and allow the cubes to "melt," about 6 minutes.

6. Fill a bowl with water and add at least 1 cup of additional pickle brine to a second. Use a slotted spoon to carefully remove the orbs from the bath, one at a time. Rinse them in the bowl of water before transferring to the brine for storage. These orbs keep up to 3 days when stored in brine.

VEGETARIAN

Mysterio's Crudités Bowl

This recipe is open-ended and designed so you can use whatever vegetables you want. My rule of thumb for an expert crudités plate or bowl is to enhance each ingredient, but only slightly. This dish is a delicious "seascape" of vegetables and there are no specific amounts you should use. We also create "sand" using maltodextrin as the base of this dish. This vegetable starch powder can be found at specialty retailers such as brewing or winemaking supply stores, or sometimes near the baking aisle or vitamin section of your local grocery store.

Cauliflower
Carrots
Olive oil
Salt
Celery
Rhubarb
Ice water
Pearl onions
Cucumber
White vinegar
Fennel
Lemon
Maltodextrin
Cumin

1. Cauliflower and carrots benefit from a little heat-based tenderizing and caramelization, with a little olive oil and salt to enhance their flavor. Notice we don't cook them to the point where they totally lose their "crudeness" (aka rawness). Set an oven to 300°F. Lay the cauliflower and carrots out on a baking sheet and drizzle a little olive oil over them. Sprinkle a little salt over the vegetables and give them a quick toss to coat before putting them in the oven for no more than 10 minutes.

2. Celery and rhubarb's texture and visual appeal can be improved by a quick slice and soak in ice water.

3. Onions, something some people despise raw, can be sweetened up by a soak with cucumbers in hot water with some salt and a splash of vinegar added.

4. Fennel gets some mechanical tenderization by slicing it thinly on a mandolin, and then its sweetness is put in check by having some salt and lemon juice drizzled on it. See what we're doing here? We aren't cooking the life out of stuff, just manipulating it or changing its appearance. *Très Mysterio, non?*

5. For the sand in this recipe, you will need maltodextrin and room-temperature fat. To keep it vegan, I used olive oil, but if you want to get wild you could use bacon fat. Just whisk the fat and maltodextrin together, adding enough maltodextrin to make a dry, sandy-feeling paste. Season it up as you'd like; I used cumin and salt. Then push it through a sieve to make your sand.

6. Finally, for full Mysterio fishbowl-head effect, sprinkle sand on the bottom of a sanitized round terrarium, then plate your veggies any way you'd like to create a beautiful seascape. Fill the terrarium with smoke using a hand smoker or by adding a tiny bit of dry ice to a ramekin of water in the center of the terrarium for a mysterious display.

Skrull Caprese Salad

YIELD: 2

Skrulls are a shapeshifting race of aliens in the Marvel Universe. One of them even married the Human Torch by disguising herself as Alicia Masters. They probably needed Matt Murdock *and* Jennifer Walters to sort out those divorce papers. To celebrate the Skrulls and their place in the universe, I wanted to create a dish that looks like one thing, but is definitely another. We do this by shapeshifting radishes to resemble mozzarella balls. This is great to bring to a work party to fool your hapless colleagues. You can find balsamic glaze at many grocery stores.

1 bunch radishes
Prepared balsamic glaze
1 pint whole cherry tomatoes
Salt
Black pepper
Extra-virgin olive oil
A few basil leaves, torn

1. Peel the whole radishes and set aside.
2. To serve, drizzle the balsamic glaze on a plate. Arrange the tomatoes and peeled radishes and season with salt, pepper, and olive oil, to taste. Garnish with torn basil leaves.

Black Widow's Charred Beet Borscht

YIELD:
2

Just like Natasha Romanoff, borscht is from Eastern Europe, and just like Natasha Romanoff, it specializes in beet-downs. To give the traditional dish a Black Widow paint job, the beets are charred to produce a matte-black soup garnished with cold beet cubes. Hard to say which is colder: frozen beets or Black Widow.

1 pound beets, unpeeled, thoroughly cleaned and sliced into rounds; plus 1 additional beet, peeled, cubed, and frozen
1 tablespoon olive oil
½ medium yellow onion, diced
2 to 3 cups chicken stock
Kosher salt, to taste
Ground pepper, to taste

1. Char the beets over an open flame. You can do this by setting an oven rack over a stove burner or by using an outdoor grill. There isn't such a thing as "too much" char here—just don't burn them to a crisp.

2. Drizzle the olive oil into a medium fry pan over medium heat and sauté the onions until they pick up some color, around 5 minutes.

3. Once the beets are charred, transfer them to a blender with 2 cups of chicken stock and the sautéed onion. For a smoother consistency, add more stock, but the "black" effect will be diminished. Blend until smooth, then add salt and pepper to taste.

4. Plate the borscht, then add the frozen beet cubes to serve.

Ironheart's Savory Oatmeal

Ironheart makes her *Eat the Universe* debut in the form of heart-healthy oatmeal with a savory twist—and we add giardiniera as a nod to Riri Williams's Chicago roots. You can find giardiniera online or in the pickle section of some grocers. In this recipe, the sauce is chile caribe, a raw chile salsa that complements almost anything savory. If you use New Mexican peppers you will assuredly taste some of the minerality (such as iron!) from the soils in which they grew. Fun fact: One of Ironheart's first adventures was in New Mexico.

2 tablespoons canola oil
½ yellow onion, finely diced
1 teaspoon ground coriander
1 teaspoon ground cumin
1 cup old fashioned oats
2 cups vegetable stock
12 dried chiles, such as New Mexican or ancho, stems and seeds removed
1 teaspoon dried Mexican oregano
3 cloves garlic, coarsely chopped
3 cups water
Kosher salt
Giardiniera for serving
Roasted sliced red and green peppers for serving
Crushed blue corn chips for serving
Sliced green onion for serving
Cilantro leaves for serving

1. Place a medium saucepan over medium heat and add the canola oil. Add the onion and cook until tender and slightly caramelized, about 7 minutes. Add the coriander and cumin and cook until aromatic, about 1 minute. Add the oats and vegetable stock and bring to a simmer. Reduce the heat to low and cook until the liquid is absorbed and the oats are tender, about 5 minutes.

2. To make the chile caribe, add the peppers to a blender along with the oregano, garlic, and water. Blend until very smooth and season with salt to taste.

3. To serve, spoon the oatmeal into bowls. Garnish with toppings as desired, and chili caribe. In the video episode I served it with prepared Italian-style beef pot roast, but this savory oatmeal is great on its own.

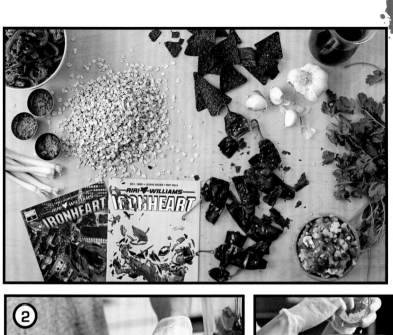

Dazzler's Pizza Bagels

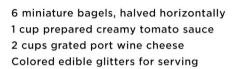

YIELD:
6

If you weren't dancing in the '80s, then you weren't really there. Dazzler sure as heck was, with her mutant power to turn the *untz untz untz* of the club into the *pow pow pow* of light blasts. I get pretty pumped up just thinking about it. Also in the '80s, if you weren't eating pizza bagels, then you weren't really there. Chronologically, if not canonically, Dazzler and this dish had to have met. This recipe is my interpretation of what that would look like. Edible glitter can be found online in myriad colors. These would be an incredible addition to any '80s-themed Marvel party.

6 miniature bagels, halved horizontally
1 cup prepared creamy tomato sauce
2 cups grated port wine cheese
Colored edible glitters for serving

1. Preheat the oven to 350°F.
2. Arrange the bagel halves on a baking sheet, cut side up. Spread a layer of tomato sauce on each, then liberally top with cheese.
3. Bake until the cheese is fully melted, about 7 minutes. Decorate with edible glitter as desired and serve.

Yancy Street Kugel

The ever-lovin' blue-eyed Thing is one of my favorite Marvel characters of all time. "It's clobberin' time" is in my repertoire of phrases, and I hope that this orange-hued, rocky-looking Jewish treat lives in your recipe repertoire. It's so easy to make even a four-fingered gargantuan like Ben Grimm could pull it off. I made the carrot juice myself with a juicer, but you can use water instead. Kugels can be sweet or savory, so adjust the sweetness and accompanying ingredients to suit your celebration. I could definitely see Human Torch bringing this to Ben and Alicia's wedding reception.

¼ cup (½ stick) unsalted butter, melted, plus more for greasing
½ pound orange-colored pasta
1 tablespoon kosher salt
8 cups carrot juice or water
6 eggs
2 cups sour cream
2 cups ricotta cheese
¼ cup sugar
2 to 3 threads saffron
1 teaspoon ground cinnamon
½ teaspoon ground cumin
½ cup dried apricots, chopped then measured

1. Preheat the oven to 375°F. Grease a 9-by-13-inch baking dish with butter and set aside.

2. Combine the pasta, salt, and carrot juice or water in a large pot and cook over medium heat until the pasta is tender, stirring frequently. Strain the pasta, allow to cool slightly, and transfer to a the prepared baking dish. Note: Don't wash the pasta! You can use the pasta liquid as a sauce for another application (I see carrot Bolognese in your future).

3. Combine the remaining ingredients in a large bowl, reserving a few apricot chunks to sprinkle on top of the kugel for garnish later.

4. Pour the egg-and-cheese mixture into the pasta in the baking dish and give it a stir to distribute the sauce. Bake for 45 to 55 minutes or until an inserted knife comes out clean.

5. Allow to cool slightly before slicing, and garnish with any additional pieces of dried apricot. Clobber.

Fantastic Four Grilled Cheese Sandwich

YIELD: 1 LARGE

If you're familiar with agar-agar, you'll know how it can make fun transparent shapes, just like Sue Storm does. Here we get to make a family favorite, grilled cheese, with four *fantastic* kinds of cheese. If you don't have craggy, Thing-like bread available, by all means use whatever you'd like.

2 green apples, peeled and chopped
2 habanero peppers, stemmed and halved
½ red bell pepper, seeded and ribs removed, coarsely chopped
1 tablespoon agar-agar
½ cup white vinegar
1 cup sugar
1 cup water
One 10-inch ciabatta loaf, halved horizontally
4 ounces sliced fresh mozzarella cheese
4 ounces Spanish goat cheese
4 ounces aged Gouda
4 ounces black truffle cheese
¼ cup (½ stick) unsalted butter

1. In a food processor fitted with the blade attachment, combine the apples, habanero peppers, bell pepper, agar-agar, and vinegar. Blend until smooth.

2. Pour into a medium saucepan lined with 4 layers of cheesecloth. Squeeze the liquid into the pot and discard the solids. Add the sugar and water and stir to combine.

3. Place the pot over medium heat and bring to a simmer, then carefully pour the hot jelly mixture into a rimmed quarter sheet pan. Refrigerate uncovered until fully set, about 1 hour.

4. When the jelly is set, preheat a panini press, or if you don't have one, set two cast-iron pans or griddles over medium-high heat.

5. Build the sandwich by layering the mozzarella, goat cheese, Gouda, truffle cheese, and the whole sheet of pepper jelly on the bottom half of the ciabatta, then top with the second half of the bread.

6. If using a panini press, butter the top and bottom of the grill, then insert the sandwich and cook until crispy on the outside and melted on the inside. If using the two-pan method, melt half the butter in one of the cast-iron pans and place the sandwich in the pan. Top the sandwich with the remaining butter and firmly press the other pan on top. Be sure not to burn yourself, as both pans are very hot. Heat, continuing to press, until cooked through. Cut in half and serve.

Ghost Rider's Formerly Fiery Fondue

As there aren't a lot of foods that taste like hellfire, motorcycles, or leather jackets, it's kinda tough to make a recipe inspired by one of Marvel's most bad-ass characters. We were able to do it on an episode of *Eat the Universe*, but what I did should never be repeated at home, lest you end up looking like a real-life version of Ghost Rider. What you have here, though, is a great recipe for fondue that looks totally awesome served in a clear, skull-shaped glass.

1 clove garlic
1 tablespoon cornstarch
1½ cups white wine, divided
1 pound Gruyère, sliced thin and cut into postage stamp–sized pieces
2 green apples, sliced, for serving
8 small purple potatoes, boiled and halved, for serving
2 slices rustic bread, cubed, for serving

1. Rub the garlic over the inside of a large stainless-steel pot, perfuming it.

2. In a small bowl, combine the cornstarch and ½ cup of the wine to create a slurry.

3. Add the remaining wine to the pot and set over medium-high heat. Bring to a simmer, then add the cornstarch slurry. Allow this mixture to come to a simmer before adding the cheese slices, a few at a time, while whisking to allow the cheese to melt evenly.

4. Once the cheese has become melty and uniform, transfer to a serving vessel and enjoy with green apple slices, purple potatoes, and slices of bread. (I'm not telling you how to do the flaming part because it's dangerous and you shouldn't do it!)

Squirrel Girl's Hot Dish

As part of the Great Lakes Avengers, Doreen Green, who has all the powers of a girl and all the powers of a squirrel, would probably enjoy this nut-tastic casserole modeled on the favorite of the northern Midwest. My favorite Squirrel Girl plot involves her single-handedly keeping Galactus at bay by steering him to a planet composed entirely of nuts. If you're a fan of Squirrel Girl, nuts, or food in general, it's a must-read.

3 tablespoons vegetable shortening, divided
1 yellow onion, diced
2 cups (7 ounces) pecans, toasted and very finely chopped
One 1-ounce package dried mushrooms, finely ground
2 cups vegetable stock
Kosher salt
1 cup water
¾ cup (4 ounces) raw almonds, soaked overnight
1 tablespoon yellow mustard
1 tablespoon soy sauce
1 tablespoon white vinegar
Shelled roasted chestnuts
Shelled toasted pistachios, chopped, for garnishing
Chopped parsley for garnishing
Chopped chives for garnishing

1. Preheat the oven to 375°F.

2. For the "ground beef," place a skillet over medium heat and add 2 tablespoons shortening. Add the onions and cook until translucent, about 7 minutes. Add the pecans and dried mushrooms and cook until slightly toasted, about 2 minutes.

3. Add the vegetable stock and scrape up any brown bits that may have accumulated in the bottom of the pan. Season with salt to taste. Bring to a simmer and cook until the pecans are tender, about 30 minutes.

4. For the "cheese sauce," combine the water, soaked almonds, mustard, soy sauce, remaining 1 tablespoon vegetable shortening, and vinegar in a blender. Blend until very smooth and season with salt to taste.

5. To assemble, spoon the nut mixture into 2 gratin or individual casserole dishes. Top with a layer of sauce, followed by the chestnuts. Bake until the centers are hot and the tops are golden brown, about 25 minutes. Garnish with chopped pistachios, parsley, and chives.

Magneto's Shakshuka

YIELD:
4

Magneto can control the forces of magnetism, and so can you with the power of an induction burner. These devices allow you to heat food without flame or exceptionally hot surfaces, all thanks to magnetics. Shakshuka is a dish that's made of a spiced tomato stew with coddled eggs. It's ideal for breakfast, but I'd never turn it down for dinner. If you don't want to unleash your magnetic might, or simply can't, by all means make this on the stove and it will be just as delicious.

2 tablespoons olive oil
1 yellow onion, diced
1 red bell pepper, seeded and ribs removed, diced
3 cloves garlic, sliced
1 tablespoon paprika
1 teaspoon ground cumin
Pinch of red pepper flakes
Pinch of ground nutmeg
One 28-ounce can whole crushed tomatoes
Kosher salt
Black pepper
6 to 8 eggs, depending on space in the pan
Cilantro for garnishing

1. Place your shiny induction burner on the counter (or just use your regular stove). Place a large skillet on the burner over medium heat and drizzle with the olive oil. Add the onions and peppers and cook, stirring occasionally, until slightly translucent and caramelized, about 15 minutes.

2. Add the garlic, paprika, cumin, red pepper flakes, and nutmeg and cook until aromatic, about 2 minutes. Add the tomatoes and cook until slightly thickened, about 15 minutes. Add salt and pepper to taste.

3. Use a spoon to make 6 to 8 evenly spaced divots in the sauce. Carefully crack 1 egg into each divot and spoon a bit of sauce around it to help keep the white contained. Cover and cook until the whites are set, about 6 minutes.

4. Top with cilantro—you can use chopped or whole leaves depending on your preference—and serve hot.

Venom's Pad See "Us"

This is a riff on a Thai dish called pad see ew, but since Venom is two characters in one—the symbiote named Venom and the human Eddie Brock—I changed the name to reflect the "us" that Venom always refers to. Here a red pepper makes for the perfect Venom tongue, while activated charcoal creates a shockingly black pasta that would probably fit right in on Klyntar. Activated charcoal can be found in health stores or online. Sweet soy sauce can be found easily online or at your local Asian market.

PASTA:
2 cups all-purpose flour, plus more for dusting
3 eggs
1 tablespoon activated charcoal
1 tablespoon soy sauce

STIR-FRY:
2 tablespoons vegetable oil, divided
1 clove garlic, minced
1 egg (optional)
8 ounces broccoli florets
2 tablespoons oyster sauce
2 tablespoons rice vinegar
2 tablespoons sweet soy sauce

TONGUE:
¼ red bell pepper

TO MAKE THE PASTA:

1. I suggest wearing gloves while handling this dough so the activated charcoal doesn't stain your hands. Place the flour on a clean work surface in a little mound. Using your fingers make a well in the center of the flour.

2. In a small bowl, whisk together the eggs, activated charcoal, and soy sauce. Gently pour this into the well, and using your fingers slowly incorporate the egg mixture into the flour. Eventually you will end up with a shaggy mess of dough. Wad this up into a ball, knead it a few times, and wrap with plastic wrap. Refrigerate the dough ball for at least 30 minutes.

3. Remove the dough from the fridge and roll it out according to the instructions on your pasta maker, or just roll out thin ropes of pasta. That's a real pasta noodle, and it's called *pici*. It's totally legit. I cut mine into more of a tagliatelle, a long, flat noodle, because it's fancy.

4. Bring a large pot of water to a boil. Boil the noodles for 4 to 5 minutes or until they are cooked al dente. Drain, then run under cold water to stop the cooking, and set aside.

TO MAKE THE STIR-FRY (OR "EDDIE BROCCOLI"):

5. In a wok or large frying pan, heat 1 tablespoon of the oil over medium heat.

6. Add the minced garlic and stir-fry until aromatic. If you'd like to add an egg to this dish, scramble and fry it in the oil, then remove, cut into chunks, and set aside.

7. Add the broccoli to the pan and stir-fry until bright green. Transfer the broccoli to a serving bowl and cover with plastic wrap to steam.

8. To make the tongue, roast the red pepper over the open flame of a gas stove until the skin is charred. Put it in a plastic bag and seal to steam for a few minutes, then rub the skin off, slice the pepper in half, and set aside.

9. Add the remaining 1 tablespoon of oil to the frying pan, allow it to heat up a bit, and then carefully add the cooked noodles, oyster sauce, and rice vinegar. Add the egg to the pan, if you made it. Toss this around until the noodles are warmed through and coated with the sauces. Drizzle with sweet soy sauce to finish. Pile the noodles on top of the broccoli, and plate on top of the noodles. "We" hope you enjoy!

Carnage's Sichuan Pasta

I remember picking up *The Amazing Spider-Man #361* and my world was never the same again. Carnage's absolutely evil demeanor and terrifying symbiote costume make Venom look like a pleasant dream. This pasta does the same with its shocking shapes and colors. I used natural coloring agents that I purchased online to achieve the look, but you can certainly use gel-based food coloring if it's easier to acquire. I also incorporated Sichuan peppercorns, which numb the palate (just like Cletus Kasady is numb to societal norms!), and Sichuan chili crisp sauce to paint the town (or plate) red. You can find the sauce in most Asian markets.

PASTA:
1 cup all-purpose flour, plus more for dusting
1 cup semolina flour
2 teaspoons salt, plus more for salting the water
¼ cup activated charcoal
¼ cup beet powder
1 cup very hot water, divided

SAUCE:
1 tablespoon rice wine or mirin
3 tablespoons Sichuan chili crisp
1 teaspoon black vinegar
1 tablespoon soy sauce

TO MAKE THE PASTA:

1. Combine the all-purpose flour, semolina flour, and salt in a large bowl. Make sure the flours are well combined, then divide the mixture between two medium bowls.

2. Add the charcoal to one bowl and the beet powder to the other.

3. Stir each bowl to combine thoroughly.

4. Make sure your hot water is very hot, then pour ½ cup into each bowl of dry ingredients. Stir each bowl separately until each mixture comes together as a shaggy dough.

5. Turn one dough out onto a floured work surface and knead for about 10 minutes. Repeat with the second dough.

6. Shape the dough into long rectangles, then use a knife to cut thin strips. Roll the strips by hand as though making a "snake" from dough-rolling days of yore.

7. Bring a large pot of salted water to a boil. Drop the pasta into the water and cook until the noodles are tender, about 5 minutes.

TO MAKE THE SAUCE:

8. Combine all the sauce ingredients in a small bowl, then toss with the noodles and serve.

DESSERT

Bifrost Cosmic Yogurt Bowls

YIELD: 2

The Bifrost, or rainbow bridge of Norse mythology, might take you to anywhere in the nine realms, but this dish inspired by it can take you almost anywhere you can imagine, at least when it comes to flavor. Most of the natural pigments used here can be found at online retailers, but feel free to use food coloring if you would like. Simply divide the yogurt into bowls, add your pigments, and paint yourself a Bifrost bowl. To make a Kirby-esque cosmos as we did in our Cosmic Yogurt Bowls episode, grab any small planetoid-looking snacks and chuck them in. Dried and fresh fruits work well to create out-of-this-world textures, while sweet and salty elements come together to engage the taste buds. Grab a spoon, and eat the yogurt universe!

2 cups Greek yogurt
Beet powder (red)
Raspberry powder (pink)
Turmeric (yellow)
Blue spirulina (blue)
Activated charcoal (black)
Mango powder (orange)
Chlorophyll (green)
Dragon fruit powder (magenta)
Various garnishes (see below)

1. The "big bang" of a cosmic yogurt universe is the Greek yogurt. That's where it all begins. The Bifrost-inspired color palette is created by adding different natural powders to the yogurt. Separate out small portions of yogurt and mix in small amounts of the powders to reach your desired colors and brightness. Some powders are more vibrant than others, so you'll have to adjust the amounts to your preference.

2. Once the colors are created, they can be spread on a plate to paint a supernova of a scene! With a nebulous yogurt setting as a backdrop, the sky is the limit when it comes to toppings. Listed below are some of the toppings we used in the video, but feel free to expand your horizons with any other interstellar edibles you may have on hand.

FRUITS:
Kiwi
Grapes
Figs
Blueberries
Starfruit
Pomegranate seeds

SNACKS:
Japanese snack mix
Peanut butter granola
Cocoa nibs
Pistachios

MISCELLANEOUS:
Candied yuzu zest
Hydrated chia seeds
Candied rose
Edible gold powder

YIELD:
4

Thena's Cold Energy Feta Frozen Yogurt

Thena is an Eternal, and I think frozen dairy products are eternally delicious. Here we get a few savory notes from the Greek cheese feta, which is fitting, as Thena was born in the Greek city of Olympia. Not to mention she can wield "cold energy" and I don't know a more fitting finish to a meal than frozen yogurt. I suggest serving this after a hefty Herculean meal of souvlaki, like the one on page 48.

4 cups Greek yogurt
½ cup powdered sugar
¼ cup honey
6 ounces crumbled feta cheese
Fresh oregano (optional)

1. In a large bowl, whisk the yogurt, powdered sugar, and honey together until combined.
2. Process the yogurt in an ice cream maker according to the manufacturer's instructions.
3. Once the yogurt has set but is not rock solid, mix in the crumbled feta. Transfer to a freezer-safe container and allow to freeze for two hours for hard-pack frozen yogurt, or serve immediately if you enjoy a softer consistency.
4. Garnish with fresh oregano for an eternally satisfying treat.

DESSERT

Ant-Man's Tiny Ice-Cream Cones

**YIELD:
4**

Whoever wears the suit—Hank Pym, Scott Lang, or Eric O'Grady—an ice-cream cone is something I doubt Ant-Man would say no to, especially an Ant-Man-sized version. This recipe requires cornet molds, which you can find at specialty bake shops or online. I find that these little cones make a great vessel for any store-bought ice cream. Whatever you do, though, don't pull a Scott Lang and steal the ice cream!

¼ cup powdered sugar
2 tablespoons unsalted butter, softened to room temperature
2 egg whites
½ cup all-purpose flour
½ teaspoon vanilla extract
Kosher salt
1 frozen raspberry
1 cup rainbow sprinkles, divided
Strawberry ice cream
Whipped cream

1. Preheat the oven to 400°F and arrange a rack in the middle of the oven. Line a small baking sheet with a silicone baking mat or parchment paper.

2. In a bowl, combine the powdered sugar and butter and stir to combine. Add the egg whites and stir until smooth. Add the flour, vanilla, and a pinch of salt and stir until smooth.

3. Portion several 2-teaspoon-size mounds of batter onto the baking mat. Moisten one finger with water and gently smooth each mound of batter into a thin, even circle, roughly 3 to 4 inches across.

4. Place in the oven and bake until the edges are barely golden brown and still pliable while hot, about 5½ minutes. Immediately roll each circle around a cornet mold and rest seam side down on a clean work surface.

5. Place the frozen raspberry in a zip-top bag. Smash with a meat mallet to break into individual drupelets, or tiny "maraschino cherries."

6. Carefully grate about 1 teaspoon sprinkles on a fine grater or rasp—or also smash these with a mallet—to make tiny sprinkles.

7. Remove the cornets from the molds. Pour the remaining sprinkles into a shallow dish and stand the cornets up in them. Fill each cornet with ice cream and top with whipped cream, tiny sprinkles, and a "maraschino cherry." Serve immediately.

She-Hulk's Vol-au-Vents

YIELD:
1

I wonder if Jennifer Walters is familiar with my work? Allegedly Jenn uses TV cooking shows to calm down after a long day as an attorney, a profession that I'm sure provides plenty of opportunities to hulk out. It's true that there is something very soothing about folding, kneading, and rolling things out, and then watching them come to life in the oven. To further soothe the stresses of She-Hulk, we add lavender, known for its calming properties, to the puff pastry, giving it a Marvel-ous scent. Dried culinary lavender can be found in many specialty food stores. And don't forget to keep an eye on the puff pastry while it's in the oven—it hulks out just like Jennifer.

All-purpose flour, for dusting
1 sheet store-bought and thawed puff pastry (or homemade is fine)
2 tablespoons dried culinary lavender leaves, divided
1 egg, beaten
Kosher salt
1 tablespoon turbinado sugar
Store-bought vanilla ice cream (or homemade is fine), for serving

1. Preheat the oven to 425°F.
2. Dust a clean work surface with flour. Lay one sheet of puff pastry on the work surface and sprinkle with a pinch of lavender. Gently press the lavender into the puff pastry using a rolling pin, dusting with flour if necessary.
3. Coat half of the puff pastry with the beaten egg using a pastry brush and fold it over the uncoated half, forming a vertical seam. Brush the exposed puff pastry with more egg wash and sprinkle with salt. Fold the puff pastry up from the bottom, forming a horizontal seam. The puff pastry should now be a rectangle.
4. Coat the exposed puff pastry with egg wash and sprinkle with lavender and turbinado sugar. Using a sharp knife, trim the edges to make a uniform rectangle with exposed edges rather than folded seams so the edges are free to expand.
5. Using a 3-inch ring cutter, cut out the center.
6. Arrange the rectangle and cut-out circle of puff pastry separately but next to one another on a parchment-lined baking sheet.
7. Bake until puffed and deeply golden brown, about 35 minutes.
8. Fill the center of the rectangle with vanilla ice cream and serve immediately, with the cut-out center beside the vol-au-vent.

Kitty Pryde's "Phasing" Gummy Candies

YIELD: VARIES

Kitty Pryde is a tough character to represent in food form, but with a little extra science we can make a fun candy that looks as if it too can phase through objects. Gels, especially those formed by hydrocolloids (no need to worry—gelatin and corn starch, two pantry staples, are hydrocolloids), work kind of like whatever material Kitty is phasing through. Kitty uses quantum tunneling (okay, now you can worry) to allow her particles to pass through a barrier. In this recipe, the gelatin forms an encasement around the liquid particles, rendering them functionally solid. My favorite trick with these gummies completes the illusion: Cut them in half, dip them in water, and affix to both sides of something vertical—a juice glass works nicely. They will look as if they are passing through the glass! I use cat-shaped molds that I found online, but any candy molds will work.

You can find candy flavoring agents online or in specialty stores. Food coloring can be found in most grocery stores. You can use any color you prefer, but I like blue and yellow, like the old-school X-Men uniforms.

Five ¼-ounce packets unflavored gelatin
⅓ cup plus ¼ cup water, divided
¾ cup sugar
½ cup corn syrup
Flavoring agent of your choice
Food coloring of your choice

1. Combine the gelatin with ⅓ cup of the water and set aside.

2. Combine the sugar, corn syrup, and the remaining ¼ cup water in a medium saucepan over medium heat. Cook until it reaches 160°F, then add the gelatin mixture and stir until dissolved, about 3 minutes.

3. Divide this mixture among however many colors and flavoring agents you decide to use.

4. Transfer the mixture(s) to squeeze bottles or carefully spoon the mixture into the molds of your choosing. Allow to rest, undisturbed and uncovered, overnight.

Nightcrawler's BAMF Cotton Candy Clouds

YIELD:
1

Kurt Wagner frequently references his time in the circus, so what better recipe than my favorite edible cloud: cotton candy. Nightcrawler's abilities and charm (and the "BAMF!" cloud he leaves behind when he teleports) are some of the coolest in the Marvel Universe. As with Kitty Pryde's "Phasing" Gummy Candies (page 130), you'll need flavoring agents, which can be acquired at specialty shops or online.

If you have a spare whisk and an electric drill or screw gun, you can make an edible version of Nightcrawler's classic BAMF clouds without a cotton candy machine. You'll need a few additional hardware elements, including tin snips (wire cutters) and a large cooler to contain the flying sugar. Always use proper safety precautions.

5 cups sugar
1⅓ cups light corn syrup
1¼ cups water
Purple food coloring
Flavored essence or candy flavoring agent of your choice

1. Using a wire cutter, snip off the round ends of a whisk to separate the tines. Insert the handle of the snipped whisk into a drill gun and tighten accordingly. Clean the interior of a large cooler and dry it thoroughly.

2. Combine the sugar, corn syrup, water, food coloring, and flavoring in a medium pot and, using a candy thermometer to watch the temperature, cook over medium heat until the temperature reaches 320°F. Transfer this mixture to a heat-safe glass bowl to stop cooking. As you are working with hot sugar, be extremely careful. Dip the tines of your new whisk-drill gun into the hot mixture, then hold the whisk so the tines are floating about halfway down into the cooler. Carefully spin the whisk in the cooler. Threads of cotton candy will be produced. Repeat the process until a large enough amount has been gathered, then enjoy.

BAMF

Nova Space-Cop Galaxy Doughnuts

**YIELD:
6**

Richard Rider adopts the mantle of Nova after being visited by the last of the Nova Corps. They are essentially space cops, doing all sorts of space things thanks to the powers granted to them through the Nova Force, generated by the living computers of Xandar. Richard Rider currently exists as Nova Prime, the highest ranking and most powerful of the Nova Corps. When I was tasked with thinking about what Richard Rider would eat after a long day of being a space cop, the answer was obvious: space doughnuts.

4 cups powdered sugar, plus more if needed
½ cup milk, at room temperature
2 tablespoons coconut oil, melted
1 tablespoon vanilla extract
Purple, black, pink, and blue gel food coloring
6 plain (unfrosted) doughnuts
Edible glitter for garnishing

1. Combine the powdered sugar, milk, coconut oil, and vanilla extract in a large bowl and whisk until uniform. If the frosting is looking too thin, add a little more powdered sugar. Divide the icing among 4 bowls.

2. Tint the icings with food coloring until the desired colors are achieved. You'll need only a few drops, as gel coloring is strong.

3. One color at a time, recombine the icings back into the first bowl and use a spatula to swirl the colors together just once. Do not over-mix or you will get a muddy color.

4. Dip the doughnuts into the swirled icing, twisting slightly to evenly coat the tops. Remove from the icing and place on a tray to rest. Sprinkle with edible glitter, if using, and let sit until the icing hardens before enjoying.

Spider-Man's NYC Cheesecake

YIELD: 8

Whether you are a Peter fan or a Miles fan, this New York cheesecake celebrates the city both web-slingers call home. You don't have to be bitten by a radioactive spider to make it; just follow the instructions. I wanted to give a nod to Miles's Caribbean heritage, so guava is used to create a web insignia on top. It also happens to be a great combination with the richness of the cheesecake, just like a Peter and Miles team-up.

CRUST:
2 cups toasted bagel crumbs
¼ cup (½ stick) unsalted butter, melted
1 tablespoon sugar

FILLING:
2 pounds cream cheese, at room temperature
8 ounces sour cream
1¼ cups sugar
1 teaspoon vanilla extract
Zest of 1 lime
¼ cup all-purpose flour
5 large eggs
Pinch of salt

GUAVA TOPPING:
1 cup guava nectar
Juice of 1 lime
1 teaspoon agar-agar
3 drops black gel food coloring
5 drops red gel food coloring

TO MAKE THE CRUST:

1. Preheat the oven to 350°F. Spray the sides and bottom of a 9-inch springform pan with nonstick baking spray and line the sides with parchment paper. Fill a kettle with water and bring to a boil.

2. In a medium bowl, combine the bagel crumbs, butter, and sugar. Press the crumb mixture into the bottom of the prepared pan and as far up the sides as possible, packing tightly with a dry measuring cup. Bake until set and lightly golden brown, about 7 minutes. Set aside to cool.

TO MAKE THE FILLING:

3. In a stand mixer fitted with the paddle attachment, beat together the cream cheese, sour cream, sugar, vanilla, and lime zest until smooth. Add the flour and mix on low until just incorporated. One by one, beat in the eggs and the pinch of salt, mixing on low between additions.

4. Wrap the outside of the prepared springform pan with aluminum foil and pour the filling into the crust. Place in a baking dish and fill with hot water halfway up the side of the pan to create a water bath.

5. Bake until the middle of the cheesecake is slightly jiggly and the top is light golden in color, about 1¼ hours. Turn the oven off and leave the door slightly open (you can put a wooden spoon in the door to keep it ajar). Let the cheesecake slowly cool in the oven for 1 hour.

6. Remove the cake from the oven and water bath and release the ring and parchment paper from the pan. Let cool completely on a rack, then cover in plastic wrap and refrigerate overnight.

TO MAKE THE GUAVA TOPPING:

7. Remove the bottom of a springform pan. Place the bottom on the counter with the lipped edge facing upward and liberally spray with nonstick spray.

8. Combine the guava nectar and lime juice in a medium pot and bring to a simmer over medium heat. Add the agar-agar and whisk vigorously. Let simmer for 1 minute longer. Turn off the heat and let cool slightly, about 3 minutes.

9. Transfer ¼ cup guava mixture to a 1-cup liquid measuring cup. Add the black food coloring and stir to combine. Pour into a squeeze bottle and set aside. Add the red food coloring to the remaining guava mixture and stir to combine.

10. Pour the red guava mixture into the sprayed springform pan bottom until almost filled. Use the black guava mixture to draw a spiral over the surface of the red topping. Using a popsicle stick, pull 8 lines from the center of the spiral to the outside to form a spider-web pattern.

11. Set aside at room temperature to set completely, about 5 minutes or more.

12. Once the topping has completely set, place a piece of parchment paper over it and invert the topping onto the paper, carefully separating it from the pan bottom without tearing it.

13. Line up the guava topping with the top of the cheesecake and invert again, parchment side up, onto the cheesecake. Carefully peel the parchment paper away and serve.

TIP: To serve, wrap a few inches of unflavored dental floss around your pointer fingers and pull taut. Slice down the center of the cake, carefully pulling one side of the floss out through the bottom of the cake after each cut. Repeat to make slices.

Green Goblin's Pumpkin Bombes

YIELD:
2

The Green Goblin was one of the first characters who caught my eye as a kid; he's the definition of *baddie*. If his green skin, weird hat, and glider weren't enough, lobbing pumpkin-shaped bombs at our friendly neighborhood Spider-Man really sealed the deal. In this recipe, we use a different kind of bomb—water balloons to give shape to our white chocolate pumpkin bombes. Bombes are a frozen dessert, and a perfect fit for Norman Osborn's second self. They even explode, with the help of a well-placed spoon strike!

7 ounces sweetened condensed milk
8 ounces canned pumpkin puree
Pinch of kosher salt
1 pound white chocolate disks
2 teaspoons orange gel food coloring
2 cups whipping cream
Cocoa nibs for serving
Toasted pumpkin seeds
Silver dragées
Green gummy candy rings

1. Fill 2 water balloons with very cold water and set aside.

2. Place a medium-heavy pot over medium-high heat and add the sweetened condensed milk. Stirring frequently, cook until lightly caramelized, about 8 minutes. Add the pumpkin puree and a pinch of kosher salt. Stir to combine and set aside to cool completely. Cover and refrigerate until ready to use.

3. Assemble a double boiler by placing 1 inch of water in a medium saucepan and placing a metal or glass bowl over it. Be sure the bowl does not touch the water. Bring the water to a simmer over medium-high heat. Add the white chocolate to the bowl and stir until melted, about 5 minutes. Add the food coloring and stir to combine.

4. Fill 2 water balloons with very cold water. Dip the balloons into the melted chocolate and let the excess drip off. Hang the balloons over a sheet tray while the chocolate sets. I recommend using clips to attach the knotted ends to a coat hanger. Once they have stopped dripping, transfer the clipped balloons to hang from a refrigerator rack until completely set, about 30 minutes.

5. Add the whipping cream to the bowl of a stand mixer fitted with a whisk attachment. You can also use a bowl and a hand mixer. Whip the cream until stiff peaks form. Add the chilled pumpkin puree mixture to the whipped cream and gently fold together to create a pumpkin mousse. Set aside.

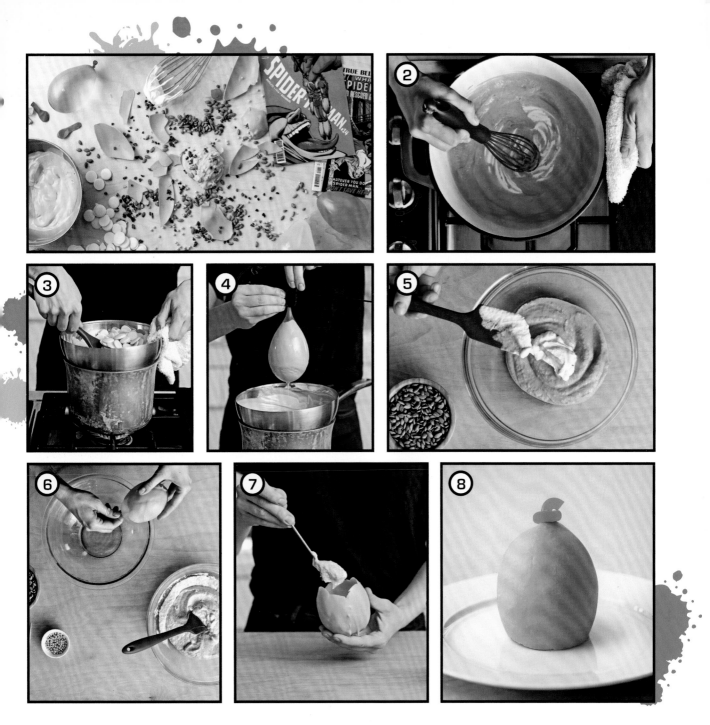

6. Remove the set chocolate balloons from the refrigerator. Use a toothpick to pierce the balloons and drain the water into a bowl. Remove any balloon scraps from the inside of the chocolate "pumpkins" and discard.

7. Trim the open edges of the chocolate pumpkins so they will sit level on a plate. Fill the pumpkins with pumpkin mousse, cocoa nibs, pumpkin seeds, and dragées. Try not to handle the pumpkins too much as the white chocolate will melt from the heat of your hand. Quickly invert each pumpkin onto a plate, open end down. Form stems out of the green gummy rings by placing a whole ring on the top of each pumpkin and then cutting another ring in half and placing each half in the hole of a ring.

8. To serve, crack open with the back of a spoon and enjoy.

MEASUREMENT CONVERSION CHARTS

VOLUME

US	METRIC
⅕ teaspoon (tsp)	1 ml
1 teaspoon (tsp)	5 ml
1 tablespoon (tbsp)	15 ml
1 fluid ounce (fl. oz.)	30 ml
⅕ cup	50 ml
¼ cup	60 ml
⅓ cup	80 ml
3.4 fluid ounces (fl. oz.)	100 ml
½ cup	120 ml
⅔ cup	160 ml
¾ cup	180 ml
1 cup	240 ml
1 pint (2 cups)	480 ml
1 quart (4 cups)	.95 liter

TEMPERATURES

FAHRENHEIT	CELSIUS
200°	93.3°
212°	100°
250°	120°
275°	135°
300°	150°
325°	165°
350°	177°
400°	205°
425°	220°
450°	233°
475°	245°
500°	260°

WEIGHT

US	METRIC
0.5 ounce (oz.)	14 grams (g)
1 ounce (oz.)	28 grams (g)
¼ pound (lb.)	113 grams (g)
⅓ pound (lb.)	151 grams (g)
½ pound (lb.)	227 grams (g)
1 pound (lb.)	454 grams (g)

ABOUT THE AUTHOR:

Despite having no formal culinary training, Justin Warner made his television debut winning Food Network's *24 Hour Restaurant Battle* at the age of twenty-six. He went on to win Season 8 of *Food Network Star*, *Cutthroat Kitchen*, and *Guy's Grocery Games*. Well known for his culinary creativity, curiosity, and enthusiasm, Justin hosts the show *Foodie Call* on FoodNetwork.com. Combining his self-described nerdiness with his love of food, Justin also hosts Marvel Comics's *Eat the Universe* on Marvel.com. Justin has written two cookbooks and has worked with many companies as a spokesperson and collaborator. According to Justin, he makes "interesting food for interested people."

ACKNOWLEDGMENTS:

I'd like to thank Jim and Mallory Viscardi, Ryan Penagos, Lorraine Cink, Judith Stephens, Jason Latorre, Jenn Manel, Larissa Rosen, Sarah Amos, Garrett Richardson, and the talent wranglers, editors, graphics people, and anyone else in the House of Ideas who has had a finger in this pie. Big thanks to the *ETU* crew and to our photographer, Alexis El Massih. Thanks to Erin Barnhart for many rounds of mutant culinary ping-pong. High praise to the team at Insight for making this project happen. Of course, without my parents encouraging me to read comic books and pursue my wildest dreams, I wouldn't be where I am. As usual, I am in debt to my gal, Brooke, for everything.

INSIGHT EDITIONS

PO Box 3088
San Rafael, CA 94912
www.insighteditions.com

f Find us on Facebook: www.facebook.com/InsightEditions
🐦 Follow us on Twitter: @insighteditions

Library of Congress Cataloging-in-Publication Data available.

ISBN: 978-1-68383-845-6

Publisher: Raoul Goff
President: Kate Jerome
Associate Publisher: Vanessa Lopez
Creative Director: Chrissy Kwasnik
VP of Manufacturing: Alix Nicholaeff
Designer: Judy Wiatrek Trum
Editor: Amanda Ng
Editorial Assistant: Maya Alpert
Managing Editor: Lauren LePera
Production Editor: Jennifer Bentham
Production Manager: Greg Steffen

Still images courtesy of the ETU team (pages 11, 13, 15, 23, 41, 51, 107, 117, 123)

All photography by Alexis El Massih

Insight Editions, in association with Roots of Peace, will plant two trees
for each tree used in the manufacturing of this book. Roots of Peace is an
internationally renowned humanitarian organization dedicated to eradicating
land mines worldwide and converting war-torn lands into productive farms
and wildlife habitats. Roots of Peace will plant two million fruit and nut trees
in Afghanistan and provide farmers there with the skills and support necessary
for sustainable land use.

Manufactured in China by Insight Editions

10 9 8 7 6 5 4 3 2 1